The book

The Bible as the foundation of the Christian faith, Greek philosophy as the basis of thought, the Age of Enlightenment as the basis of scientific knowledge - the three pillars of today's view of the world. That philosophy began with the ancient Greeks is just as invented as the myth of the Sea Peoples, who ushered in the end of the Bronze Age. Nor does the story of the Flood originate from the Bible.

The Age of Enlightenment not only destroyed a medieval view of the world, but at the same time created new myths that are rarely questioned even today.With a good portion of irony, the stories are scrutinised and filleted. Where they come from and since when they have been told holds the one or other surprise.

We accompany the first archaeologists to Nineveh and take part in a Greek symposium with Herodotus. We meet Rousseau in Annecy and learn what 'Haute Cousine' and 'Guillotine' have in common. We attend Hegel's lectures in Berlin and accompany Wallace to Borneo.

From Noah to Kant, from Uruk to Ulm, from Cinderella to flying orangutans, the stories are so numerous that one or two souvenirs are likely to remain from this journey through time.

The author

Stefan Brill (1967) is a political scientist, economist and holds a PhD on philosophy. He was living in Central America, Europe and Asia, but now prefers to spend his time at his home in the sunny south, hoping not to lose too much money on the stock market again.

ša nagba imuru

or

He who saw the abyss

An extraordinary journey through the stories of our thinking

Bibliographic information of the German national library:
The German national library lists this publication in the Deutsche Nationalbibliografie; detailed bibliographic data are available on the Internet at dnb.dnb.de

Production and publishing: BoD – Books on Demand, Norderstedt

ISBN: 9783754344859

Invitation

Feel invited to join a colourful journey through time, enjoying a number of very beautiful stories. A number of them are extremely old, but surprisingly actual, some may sound completely ridiculous, some are absurd in deed, an some are true simply because they are believed to be so. And yet they are nothing but entertaining stories.

It is an entertaining journey to places one would not have guessed what happened there and to the days in which they were invented. They are often marvellous stories, that still shape our ideas of the world today. However, when asking for their origins and since when they were told, one often receives a surprising answer.

Join in, if you got curious. It's just another story which you may believe or not. Get on board, we're heading for

... Bodenwerder!

Content

Greek stories

Don't trust in swans with morning glory
Woman with Stockholm syndrome – Hellenic fantasies
Farting philosophers – Pre-Socratic lifestyle – Bizarre deaths in philosophy - Herodotus in Bodenwerder
Greek Symposium – Athenian triumvirate

Stories of a new time

Hermann der Lame – Confessions of a late riser
The story of the new thinking - Falling Stones
Heaven on earth - Let there be light – Royal droppings
I stink therefore I am - Bouillon Rectal - Lac du Annecy
Story of the Haute Cuisine - Interesting Times

Fabricated Stories

Archangel Francesco - Göttingen makes history
An unfinished age - Cocktail Fatal – The story of the German Greeks - Dessert with bad taste

Stories from Islands

Present Not Voting - Enlightenment in a kilt
Abyss of time - Homo Diluvii Testis - About giraffes
Sailing the Pacific - The story of the flying Orang-Utan
Welcome to the Bermuda triangle
The Malayan archipelago – Of flatheads and big beans

He who saw the Abyss

Of false rabbits and mouse-dogs - Ark of a Dream

A castle in Bodenwerder

'Liar, liar, pants on fire'

Many may be familiar with the outrages tall tales of Baron Munchhausen, in which he mounted a cannon ball and let himself shot over a town, changed saddles in the air, and flew right out again on another ball.

Although the Baron's stories were probably a tiny little bit exaggerated, only few people know that this Hieronymus Carl Friedrich Freiherr von Munchhausen was in fact a very real person. The Hanoverian storyteller very much enjoyed to tell his stories to a small, very private audience at his 'castle' in Bodenwerder.

Baron Munchhausen was one of the 'Brunswick Cuirassiers' sent by his sovereign to serve in Russia, from where he not only brought back his wife, but also some old gold coins with the coinage of Ivan III. When some time later Tsarina Elisabeth came to power, she let destroy everything that reminded of her predecessor, including the coins with the portrait of the previous ruler. Munchhausen, thus, came unexpectedly into possession of a rare treasure of his time, which soon would cause him some serious trouble.

He fared quite well after his return from the east, living quietly and contentedly on his small country estate for decades and enjoyed the best health. The baron was a marvellous storyteller, and soon his anecdotes were circulating all around Bodenwerder.

One of his most attentive listeners was Rudolf Raspe, a true polymath and 'bon vivant', who was interested in everything that was fashionable at the time. This not only included the baron's coin collection, but also his new young wife. Some time after becoming a widower, the old baron had fallen foolishly in love with his only twenty years old goddaughter Bernhardine Brunsig von Brunn. Money and young women have driven many elderly gentleman to ruin, and Munchhausen was not to be spared. What all this has to do with Mr Raspe is probably known to only very few.

Rudolf Raspe was a typical child of the Enlightenment, had studied at Göttingen, later became the curator at the Ottoneum in Kassel and was even elected to the highly respected Royal Society in England.

Things were actually going very well for him, except that his private expenses as a 'bon vivant' did not quite correspond with his income as a curator. He could not resist, and it was only a matter of time when he was charged with stealing from the Landgrave's gem collection. He fled to England, wanted by the police as a 'red-haired man of medium height'.

Installing himself in London and suffering from a constant money shortage, Raspe remembered the Baron's tall tales and soon published them under the title 'Baron Munchausen's Narrative of his Marvellous Travels and Campaigns in Russia'. The book became a bestseller and the first editions were quickly sold out. His success however, had fatal consequences for the actual baron himself.

For the Munchhausens, the ideas of marriage were understandably not exactly equivalent. What the baron expected to be his last love affair, his fifty years younger wife regarded more as a care facility for senior pensioners in need. Of course, young Bernhardine, very soon needed a little money for a rather comprehensive cure in the spa of Bad Pyrmont.

Raspe seized his chance, visited the young woman and thus came into possession of the baron's valuable coin collection for little money. Whatever may be understood by a 'comprehensive cure', it was an extremely fruitful period for Bernhardine. Nine months later, her daughter was born, and it cannot be ruled out entirely that Raspe was somehow connected with this.

To the old baron it was immediately clear that he was cheated and not to be held responsible for this 'accident'. He immediately accused his young wife of adultery and filed for divorce. In the long lasting divorce proceedings, his newly acquired title as the 'Lying Baron' took its revenge.

His heavily pregnant wife accused him in court that all his accusations were fabrications. As proof, she presented the stories that Raspe had circulated. The judges finally believed the young wife, and so the baron's last adventure ended in a financial fiasco.

Of course, this story had to begin with Baron Munchausen, with him and a university that is just being founded. It was his uncle, Gerlach Adolph Freiherr von Munchhausen, Prime Minister to King George II, who established the University of Göttingen in 1734 in the name of his Majesty, from which Rudolf Raspe graduated a few years later.

It was soon to become a globally respected institution, where figures such as the English crown princes, the Humboldt brothers, the brothers Grimm, a Baron von Stein, and many others were to study.

'*My whole trust rested on men like Heyne, Michaelis and many others; my most ardent wish was to sit at their feet and take note of their teachings*', wrote Johann Wolfgang Goethe, a contemporary of the Baron and probably one of the most influential literary figure a few years later.

The uncle of the 'Lying Baron', Gerlach Adolph Freiherr von Munchhausen, soon brought the very professors Goethe mentioned here to his new university. Michaelis was to become one of the first 'Orientalists', and Heyne the most famous Greek scholar of his time.

We will soon find out what this university was all about and what significance it had. But let us finally begin our story. Let's start out journey and travel to a small park in nearby Göttingen...

The beginning of the Story

A walk in the park
Coitus Interruptus in Arabia
Coffee black as ink
Rendezvous in Baghdad
Bel-Air in Persia
The bet

A walk in the park

Welcome to the famous city of Göttingen. Let's take a seat on one of the benches near by and let us enjoy a moment of silence in the warming summer sun. We are still quite undisturbed, as the new century has only just begun. The nineteenth, to remind you.

Just around the corner comes a young student named Georg Grotefend, arguing with his fatherly friend Fiorillo about what has just happened in the world outside.

It was the Age of Enlightenment, and people were well aware of it. For those who were not, a certain Immanuel Kant, who was known all over the place already, was blaring out from Königsberg to his listeners that they should switch on their brains for a change and free themselves from their 'self-incurred immaturity', as he called it.

> *'Enlightenment is man's emergence from his self-incurred immaturity'*, he said.
> *'Immaturity is the incapacity to use one's mind without the guidance of another. Such immaturity is self-incurred if it is not caused by lack of understanding, but by lack of determination and courage to use one's mind without being guided by another.*
> *Sapere Aude! Have the courage to use your own mind is therefore the motto of the enlightenment'.*

Slowly, people began to realise why the world was the way it was. Mankind began after the Deluge, and wisdom came with the Greeks. That's how it was written, that's how it was told, and that's how it had to be.

However, the world was changing rapidly. Before Georg was born, there was order. In France, the king carried his head on his shoulders and sat firmly on the throne. Louis XVI was France, France was great, and Paris was the centre of the world. Now, chaos had broken out. The king was found below the guillotine and his head in the basket in front of it. Together with his head the whole old order seemed to have fallen.

Everywhere in the Holy Roman Empire of German Nations, the 'Reich', there was talk of 'citizens', of a 'nation', and of 'freedom and equality' that had come with the revolution. Many were waiting for Napoleon, who had just returned from Egypt. In the salons and at the universities there was no other topic than the French Revolution, and many wished that the Frenchman would finally come, and with him the long desired change.

Georg had some serious difficulties with this kind of thinking. His sovereign was George III, King of England and Ireland, and German 'Kurfürst', the Duke and Prince-elector of Brunswick-Lunenburg. Which nation should one belong to?

England used to be a dwarf, but now it was rapidly developing into a world power. George III owned colonies all over the world, from America to India. Steam engines fogged entire cities and drove the 'industrial revolution'. The economy was the hot topic on the island and new factories mushroomed everywhere. There was a huge rumble in Europe at the moment.

Georg Grotefend tried to escape from all these new developments. He was interested in ancient history, a rather new topic at his University. Over the past few weeks, he had been searching through the archives of the library and found some old travel reports from the Orient. In the reports were drawings of ancient ruins, and on these ruins was an ancient script that no one had yet been able to decipher. Well, to be honest, no one was really interested in it, and no one could only imagine, that these few lines held the key to an extraordinary treasure.

Absolutely no one could have foreseen that these ancient characters of a long forgotten language would soon contribute to the collapse of an entire world view. How these reports with its ancient inscriptions came into the possession of his University is again a story of coincidences.

Coitus Interruptus in Arabia

Some forty years ago, the above mentioned Professor Michaelis had managed to set up the first really scientific research expedition to Arabia. Actually, it was failed expedition, and the professor had not taken any further notice of the results. Now, Georg had rediscovered the report of that journey in the dusty realms of the university library.

When initiating the expedition, the old professor wanted to check what was true about the stories in the Bible. He had no doubt about the Holy Scriptures, not at all. One was living in the age of enlightenment, the age of reason, and no one of sound mind doubted the Scriptures of God, the creation and the deluge. There was absolutely no reason to do so.

Michaelis was rather looking for scientific evidence for the authenticity of the Bible. So, what could be more obvious than sending someone to Arabia to check the informations set out in the Scriptures?

Like many of his colleagues, the professor believed that Arabia had not changed very much since biblical times. So he sat down, picked up his Bible and wrote down all the questions that seemed to be of importance.

There were questions about the climate, the cities and landscapes, about the animals that were living, and the plants that could be found there. Specifically, he was interested in where the Red Sea got its colour from, whether there were flying snakes, how the manna was prepared, or whether the Arabs, like the Hottentots, lined up their oxen with their horns close together for protection against wild animals.

The ideas about the Orient were, to put it mildly, still somewhat simple-minded, if not gawkish. Most likely, the professor had never left northern Europe and drew his knowledge mainly from the bible. Many of his colleagues were no different.

Michaelis summarised all these important questions in a book, 'Questions for the Society of Wise

Men', a veritable cabinet of delicacies. The professor asked whether toothaches were less frequent in Arabia, and what this had to do with warm coffee. Or whether 'uncircumcised' men were more often plagued by carbuncles in the warm climate of Arabia than 'circumcised' men, and what the whole thing had to do with skin colour. Of course, he was also interested in the different types of emasculation, especially whether the 'testicles were squeezed out or the rut was cut off'. Michaelis knew his Bible by heart, and there it says that: '*He whose testicles are crushed or whose male member is cut off shall not enter the assembly of the Lord*' (Deut. 23.1).

He was also interested in ancient customs and was wondering, whether the despised sister-in-law was still allowed to pull off her brother-in-laws shoe and spit him in the face calling him '*the man that had his sandal pulled off*'. What seems to us rather odd today was a perfectly understandable and normal question for that time. You only need to know the biblical story of Judah and Tamar, which goes as follows:

Tamer had married Judah's eldest son Ger, and both seem to have lived happily together. However, they had not yet produced a male offspring when Ger suddenly suddenly died. Without a son, however, the widow was left without inheritance, so her father--in-law sent his second son Onan to take care of the matter. The two tried their very best, but whenever the time came, Onan preferred to drop the semen on the floor, says to the Bible. This first 'coitus interruptus' in worlds literature did not please the Lord at all, and so Onan had to die, too.

Interestingly, however, 'onanism' today is synonymous with 'masturbation', with which the biblical Onan had nothing whatsoever to do. The 'coitus interruptus' on the other hand, to which Onan ultimately fell victim, is still considered the only permissible method of contraception in many Christian religious circles. Actually, a completely upside down interpretation of the words of the Bible, but that's the way it is with many religions. But let's go back to the story.

Tamer was still without an heir and waiting for son number three to finally produce a male offspring with her. Little Shelah, that was his name, was obviously not yet ready for such experiences, and so Papa Judah soon forgot to fulfil his obligation. Obviously, Tamer was less enthusiastic about this and figured out a plan on how to get what she deserved.

So she disguised herself as a prostitute by putting on a headscarf - it seems to have been that easy in those days – and this heavily masqueraded, she sat down outside the city waiting for her father-in-law. He actually came along, did not recognize her, of course, booked her for one night, paid, got her pregnant, and left satisfied the next morning. That's the way, Tamer finally got her heir, so it is written in the Bible, and that's how it had to be (Genesis 38).

So far so good, but there is still the matter of the 'shoe-thing', and of course, it is also part of the Bible stories. If the brother refuses to go to bed with his sister-in-law, which may well occur in real life, then:

'his brother's wife shall go up to him in the presence of the elders, and pull his sandal off his foot, and spit in his face; and she shall answer and say, 'So shall it be done to the man who does not build up his brother's house.' And the name of his house shall be called in Israel, The house of him that had his sandal pulled off.' (Deut. 25:9-10).

Wonderfully absurd things are written in the Scriptures, but let us return to our story. Equipped with a whole catalogue of such unintentionally weird questions, the expedition set out by ship from Copenhagen on 4 January 1761. It consisted of six former students from Göttingen University, among them a certain Carsten Niebuhr.

The notes of this gentlemen tell us of a total fiasco of the expedition right from the beginning. Soon after the departure they were hit by strong winter storms, the sailors were blown out of the masts and died like flies. It finally took them nine months before they arrived in Egypt, from where the six expedition members made their way to 'Arabia Felix', to the south of the Saudi Arabian peninsula.

They expected to find the 'original' way of biblical life, almost unchanged for centuries. What they encountered were 'original' swarms of malaria mosquitoes that attacked the completely perplexed and unprepared travellers and feasted on them in the best possible manner.

In May, the first participant, Friedrich Christian von Haven, died of malaria in Mokka, six weeks later Peter Forskal on the way to Sanaa. The survivors decided to leave for Bombay by ship, but two more participants, Baurenfeind and Berggren, died while still at sea. When the expedition arrived in India in September 1763 - after just one year of effective exploration - four of the six participants had already died. The British East India Company had just driven its French competitors from the subcontinent during the Seven Years' War. India was now one of the colonies of the English king, who was also the founding father of the University of Göttingen, which finally explains the destination India.

In Bombay, however, also the last travelling companion died, and Niebuhr decided to travel alone and anonymously under the name 'Abdallah' for the next four years. Slowly the last survivor realized, that the ideas of his professor had little to nothing in common with reality.

The Arabs, noted Niebuhr, had less toothache not so much because they consumed hot coffee, but because they simply cleaned their teeth after every meal. In general, he no longer seemed to think much of Michaelis and his catalogue of questions.

> '*If it is true that the oxen of the Hottentots are accustomed to stand close together in a row at night in order to oppose the incoming wild animals with a whole line of horns (Michaelis 46th question), then the Arab oxen must be more stupid, for I have never heard of such virtues from them*', he noted.

Niebuhr wrote down and mapped everything he saw. When he finally reached the ruins of Persepolis in March 1765, he made some drawings, including a detailed copy of a script that no one in Europe had yet been able to read.

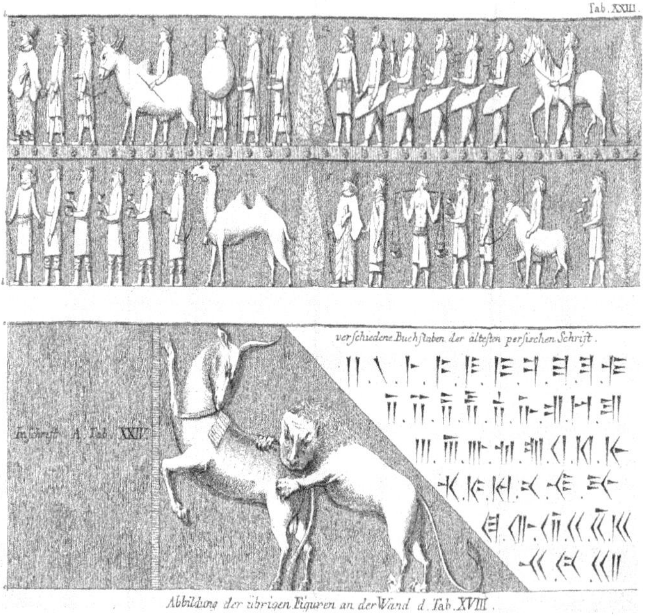

'Of the beautiful wedge-shaped script, one finds almost constantly three inscriptions of three different alphabets next to each other... The seal may perhaps be useful to the linguist; for the animal it contains is certainly a mythical animal of the Persians, and thus the writing around it is likewise Persian', he noted in the report.

Niebuhr passed by Mosul, but had no idea of the archaeological treasures under the hills not far from the city. When he finally returns home in 1767, all his notes were in vain.

Disappointed that the reports did not meet his expectations, Professor Michaelis declared the expedition a failure, and many of his maps and drawings ended up in the library archives. It were these records that Georg Grotefend encountered when digging through the depths of his university's library.

In addition, there were three other books that the young student had come across that gave certain clues to the ancient history of Mesopotamia. One by an old Augsburg 'medico', another by an Italian nobleman, and finally one by a Parisian jeweller. All three wonderful stories, which shall therefore be told briefly.

Coffee black as ink

The first book was was written by a German doctor entitled: Leonhart Rauwolf's 'Actual Description of the Journey which he himself made before this time towards the Orient, namely Syria, Judea, Arabia, Mesopotamia, Babylonia, Assyria, Armenia, and not without little trouble and great danger: besides reporting many strange and memorable things, all of which he inquired about, saw and observed'.

In 1582 books still bore titles that unequivocally revealed what they were about. More than a hundred years later, when book titles already became much shorter, the English title decreased to a simple: '*Dr. Leonhart Rauwolf's Travels into the Eastern Countries*' for its English translation in 1693.

Rauwolf was an expert in medicinal herbs from Augsburg, and fulfilled a childhood dream with his journey in 1573. The Orient with its knowledge of medicine and medicinal herbs had fascinated him for a long time. When his brother-in-law's trading company was looking for someone to provide more information from Arabia that Leonhardt took the chance of his life.

His journey lasted about three years, and he was probably one of the first Europeans to describe the pleasure of a hot coffee: '*A very good drink they call Chaube that is almost as black as ink and very good in illness, especially of the stomach*'.

Leonhardt describes the Tower of Babel as a castle mountain with a ruined fortress '*near which stood the Babylonian high tower, which the children of Noah (who first inhabited this land after the Flood) began to build up to heaven*'.

For Leonhardt it is the biblical landscape and was the first inhabited land after the deluge. It was probably the first time a traveller described the reasonably correct location of biblical Babylon in a book.

He also passes through Mosul and notices the beautiful hilly landscape, unaware of the archaeological treasures that lied buried beneath. Today, however, Rauwolf is known less for his description of the Tower of Babel than for the Rauwolf plants named after him.

Rendezvous in Baghdad

Georg had found another clue to the cuneiform script in the travelogue of Pietro della Valle. It is not only the diary of an unusual journey at a time when Europe was heading straight for the Thirty Years' War, when witches were burned on funeral pyres and superstition was booming. It is also an eerily beautiful love story of two persons who could not have been more different.

Pietro della Valle was a young nobleman in his late twenties when he fell head over heels in love with an *'exceedingly beautiful lady, from whom he had the certain and sincere promise of her fidelity, but was deceived'*, writes Abbot Filippo Maria Bonini in the description of della Valle's life. The Abbot describes his character as of

> *'moist and warm temperament, which, because it was in great excess in him, caused him to think highly, briskly resolute in his business, and exceedingly fierce in his sensual performance for why he took everything else for a joke and threw it to the winds'.*

What this moist temperament is all about is probably left to the reader's imagination, but the fact that he doesn't take life too seriously and rather as a big joke makes della Valle a very likeable character. Bonini's character description is simply delicious. It is the language of the lush and sultry baroque that is presented here.

In Naples, della Valle initially tried to gain distance from the gruelling thoughts of his lost love affair. Finally, his friend Schipano advised him to make a pilgrimage to Palestine to forget his heartbreak. He had no idea in 1614 that his friend would now be travelling for almost 12 years and his journey will bring him as far as to India.

Pietro regularly sends his 'missives' to his friend, and is almost ready to return home to Italy when he falls in love with an extremely beautiful but completely unknown Aurora, whom he knows only by reputation. Pietro writes his friend:

> '*that in this country the rumour of the beautiful Aurora has reached my ears, that I am compelled, out of fervent desire to see her, even to possess her, to take in hand another journey, not so long, but just as long and arduous, and then no less strange*'.

The very next day he sets off for Baghdad, quickly describes the Tower of Babel and the lion's den into which Daniel was thrown, and finally meets his Aurora, who turns out to be Sitti Ma'ani Gioerida.

> '*She is Assyrian by birth, sprung from ancient Christian blood, about eighteen years old, and, besides her gifts of mind, which are quite uncommon in her person, of such pleasing bodily form that, if it were not indecent for a husband to praise his wife, I might well*

say, without glorification, that she was worthy of love'.

Yes, you read quite right, 'veni, vidi, nupsi', the old Latin would say, I came, saw and got married. Almost on arrival he is wedding his beloved Aurora, whom he had never seen before. By now, at the latest, he had forgotten all his Italian despair and pain, and cannot stop romanticizing about his new wife:

'The length of her body is neither too long nor too short for a woman's image, but her whole body in all parts is in stately proportion, together with her lovely gracefulness, noble gestures, and wondrous pleasantness when she speaks, and still more when she smiles, and lets her small and snow-white teeth be seen, and other such circumstance, in which I fell in love'.

This is how a young Italian nobleman of a Baroque 'moist and warm temperament' writes about his young wife. Both were travelling together for the following years and also reached Persepolis, where della Valle made the first documented copy of the cuneiform script. It is for these few lines that he would later enter the history books. However, he had no clue about it.

Already on the way back to Italy, his Ma'ari died of a fever, and when Pietro della Valle arrived back in Rome after a twelve-year journey, he had in his luggage not only a few souvenirs, the copies from Persepolis with the strange cuneiform writing, but also the mummified body of his deceased and dearly beloved wife, which he had buried in the family tomb.

Pietro was indeed a rum one, but a very likeable and sympathetic one.

Bel-Air in Persia

The last book with references to cuneiform writings that Georg had found was the report of a jeweller's son from France named Jean Chardin. He had learned his trade in his father's shop in the Place Dauphine in Paris.

When he was born in 1643, the Thirty Years' War was already over and the only five-year-old Louis XIV, the later 'Sun King', was sitting on the French throne while civil war was just breaking out in England. At that time, France was developing into a major European power and expanding its colonies and trade relations all over the world, including the East Indies. Also the French king had colonies in India at this time, although it sometimes seems to have been forgotten.

Chardin was only twenty-one years old when his father became a shareholder in the newly founded Compagnie des Indes Orientales, the French East India Company. The father immediately sent his son to Persia to establish new trade relations. The young man quickly became court jeweller to the Persian king and brought home several copies of the cuneiform script from Persepolis. Twenty-six more books with this ancient cuneiform are said to be in Isfahan, he wrote in his book 'Journal du Voiages du Chevalier Chardin en Perse'.

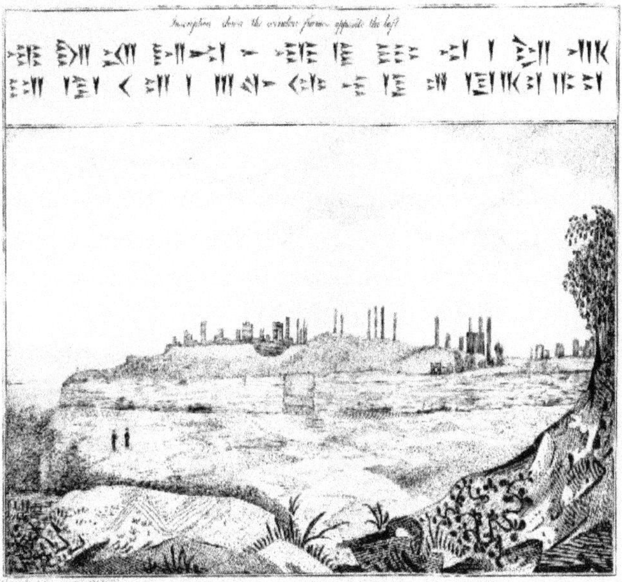

PERSEPOLIS FROM THE SOUTH

And while the plague hit hard on London and King Charles II fled London with his family and took up residence in Oxford with the entire court in 1665, young Chardin raved about the pure air in faraway Persia.

'The air is cool in this country, and this cool air has the wondrous property that the people, except on the borders towards the south and north, are altogether very healthy,

beautiful in colour, and of both sexes of body strength, limber and shapely', he noted. A bid of fresh air can work out wonders and is extremely good for ones health. It was already known hundreds of years ago.

The bet

Let's return to the university in Göttingen, where Georg Grotefend had been discussing for hours with his friend Fiorillo all that he had found in the bowels of the library. Deciphering ancient writings was en-vogue at this time, but no one was interested in the ancient cuneiform that Georg had found in the dusty corridors of the university library.

To put an end to the whole discussion, Fiorillo proposed a wager to his youthful friend. If he actually managed to decipher the signs, Georg would receive his first scientific publication. This was, of course, a challenge the young student accepted immediately. A short later, in the summer of 1802, he locked himself in his student room, sat down in front of his overcrowded desk, took the ancient cuneiform inscriptions, and began his work.

What experts need years for, Georg solved the puzzle within only a few weeks and was actually able to decode about a third of all the yet completely unknown cuneiform characters. In September 1802, he presented his groundbreaking findings to the professors of the university, and what followed this sensation was... absolutely nothing!

The scientific community took almost no notice of him and his findings. He received an encouraging pat on the back, and that was the end of his steep scientific career. Georg Grotefend was the right man, in the right place, but unfortunately at the wrong time.

Georg had found a key to a secret that was still buried under metre-thick layers of collapsed clay ruins near Mosul. He was not to experience the actual sensation, which had to do with a young Englishman standing stark naked in the British Museum. But we'll get to that story later.

In the meantime, we have to do a little archaeology, a completely new field of research that didn't exist until now. The cuneiform texts that Georg translated so far really didn't give too much away, but that was soon to change. The explosive power that was associated with it is hardly imaginable today.

So let's say goodbye to Göttingen for now. We will now join two of the most famous 'archaeologists' who excavated the ancient ruins in Mesopotamia. They probably made their finds more by mere chance and due to infinite boredom, but have a look for yourself.

Let's go to France, at a time when Napoleon was already history...

Excavated Stories

Ninive retrouvée
Ashurbanipal's library
Naked at the museum
The Babel-Bible-Controversy

Nineveh retrouvée

In early nineteenth-century Europe, the vast majority of people were absolutely convinced of the validity of the Bible. The stories of the divine creation were considered universally accepted, and the biblical accounts of the Assyrians, the Babylonians and the Egyptians in no way doubted. There were, however, some few scientists who claimed that something might not be quite right with the whole story, but with minor modifications even these observations could be brought in line with the Bible. There was no real reason to be alarmed in any way.

Moreover, since Napoleon's campaign to Egypt in 1798, vast quantities of ancient Egyptian inscriptions had been brought back to France, which were now gradually being deciphered. The Frenchman Champollion was the first to be able to correctly interpret the ancient Egyptian hieroglyphs, and the events described in the deciphered texts often corresponded to the accounts in the Bible.

What was missing, however, was real evidence from Mesopotamia, where the ancient empires of Assyria and Babylonia must have been located, where Abraham came from, and where Noah survived the Deluge. Mesopotamia was the origin of man, so it was said in the Bible, and the Bible speaks the truth, people were convinced. So, t was time to take a closer look at the region and search for evidence.

Let's go on board the 'Heros', a French merchant ship, where we will meet the first protagonist of this story. After departure from France, the ship headed south to the Atlantic, circumnavigated Cape Horn, and cruising northwards to California. Even the captain, August Bernard Duhaut-Cilly, did not know exactly what the hell they were doing here. He had been trying to sell his merchandise for two years, constantly sailing back and forth between Hawaii and San Francisco.

Out of pure boredom, the young doctor on this ship, Paul-Émile Botta, had already started compiling a French-Hawaiian dictionary. Of course, Botta had no idea that he would one day find the biblical Nineveh while sailing in paradise on the other end of the world. When he finally returned to France after three years, he was probably just as ignorant as the young Charles Darwin, who was soon to set off for the Pacific with the 'Beagle'.

Many great discoveries, one might assume, are made out of sheer boredom. Years later, when Botta became consul in Mosul, it seems, he must have got heavily bored again. This time, however, he did not start with a dictionary, but grabbed a spade and dug through the beautiful hills outside the city to the east of Mosul. It was the year 1842.

As it soon turned out, these beautiful hills, called 'tells', were not just natural elevations, but nothing more than the overgrown remains of long-decayed cities. Botta quickly found the first shards, but unfortunately his companion convinced him to continue digging further north. There was much more to be found there, he told the Frenchman, and so Botta set off north and continued his work there. He had just discovered the long-sought Nineveh, and then carelessly left it behind. Of course he did not have the faintest idea at the time.

As soon as he started with his new excavation north of Mossul, he was immediately successful. Just below the surface, he came across palace walls decorated with reliefs and inscriptions in cuneiform writing. At the main entrances were huge winged bull sculptures almost five metres high.

'I believe I am the first to have discovered sculptures which, it may be supposed, belong to that period when Nineveh was in its prime' Botta noted in his book. He was so excited and overwhelmed that he telegraphed to France: 'Ninive etait retrouvée' - Nineveh has been found.

The problem, however, was that no one had yet been able to decipher the cuneiform inscriptions that were now being found all over the ruins. Georg Grotefend's discovery had not interested anyone at the time, otherwise Botta would have known intermediately, that it was not Nineveh but Dûr-Sharrûkin, the palace of Sargon II, he discovered.

On one of the clay tablets that were excavated, the following was written in cuneiform: '*Sargon, king of the universe, built this city: Dûr-Sharrûkin is its name; within it he had this incomparable palace built*'. It's that simple sometimes in archaeology, you just have to be able to read.

Anyway, Botta had everything packed into boxes and sent it to the Louvre, triggering a veritable stampede in Paris. Everyone wanted to see with their own eyes what was left of Nineveh. The Bible tells the truth, people were convinced, and there was no doubt about it.

A short time later, however, when the cuneiform writing was finally completely deciphered and the error was discovered, this only fuelled the enthusiasm even more. Suddenly there was clear scientific proof. After all, the Holy Scriptures read: '*In the year that the commander in chief, who was sent by Sargon the king of Assyria, came to Ashdod and fought against it and took it...*' (Isaiah 20.1). So the Bible was right, Sargon really existed, and Botta had discovered his palace.

However, just before Botta could set out to correct his mistake and seek the right Nineveh, he got caught up in the mills of politics. After the February Revolutions of 1848, he lost his post in Mosul and had no other choice but to observe Austen Henry Layard doing his job.

So it is time to visit the other great archaeologist. Let's go to London, where a very depressed young lawyer is sitting at his desk, about to shoot a bullet in his brain out of deadly dullness. A good indication that a great discovery is about to be made. In fact, the life of this young man was going to change so drastically that it almost knocked him off his feet. He just had to wait for a Mr Mitfort to finally get going.

Ashurbanipal's Library

Austen Henry Layard was certainly not the kind of person who liked to stay at home as a young man. Well, he didn't like to stay in one place in his later years neither, and making his living in his uncle's lawyer's office wasn't exactly an appealing idea of his future lifestyle.

Layard was born in 1817 in a hotel in Paris, a circumstance that might have had a decisive influence on his later life. He grew up in Florence, Geneva and in France, and was later sent to boarding school in England at the age of twelve. Some ten years later he finally became a lawyer in his uncle's office and understandably quite depressed.

His opportunity for a life as an adventurer and explorer only arose when an acquaintance of his uncle, Edward Mitfort, was looking for a companion to travel to Ceylon to set up a coffee plantation. Only, Mitfort had a panic fear of water, so he wanted to go all the way to India by land. Layard was thrilled to finally get out of the stuffy office.

They both decided to take only the bare essentials, and those were some double-barrelled pistols, a compass, a sextant and a bed. It is somewhat amusing to imagine the two travellers arriving in Mosul in April 1840, observing the great 'tells' on the east bank of the Tigris - with their bed on their back. However, south of Mosul they passed by a stately hill in the shape of a pyramid, which reminded Layard to the story of the old Greek Xenophon, who must have come along here some two thousand years ago.

Xenophon was a pupil of the famous philosopher Socrates and took part in a battle against Atraxerxes II with ten thousand Greek mercenaries in 401 B.C. Of course he wrote a book about his heroic deeds entitled

'Anabasis'. The background were disputes over the succession to the Persian king Darius II. His younger son Cyrus had gathered troops in Asia Minor, including ten thousand Greek mercenaries, to march against his older brother Artaxerxes II, who was in Babylon. Unfortunately, Cyrus was killed in battle north of Babylon, and so it fell to Xenophon to lead the Greek mercenaries back home.

The fact that he left behind the entire entourage of wives and children, prostitutes, catamites and jugglers, blacksmiths, butchers, bakers, millers and whoever else, does not detract from his heroic deed, of course. After all, Xenophon wrote the book himself.

In any case, these ten thousand mercenaries moved north along the Tigris, and Xenophon reports of a deserted city that had previously belonged to the Medes, with huge ring walls and impregnable. '*Near the city was a stone pyramid, one plethron wide, two plethrons high*', Xenophon writes in his book.

Layard never made it to Ceylon. For two years he vagabonded more or less aimlessly through the Middle East, became entangled in political intrigues, was attacked and got robbed several times, and finally stood half-naked with bleeding feet and without a bed at the city gate of Baghdad, where he collapsed unconscious.

After his uncle also stopped his alimony payments, the young man was literally stuck in Mesopotamia. By sheer coincidence the British consul in Istanbul was just looking for an 'assistant' for special diplomatic purposes, and it took Layard several years before he finally got the opportunity and sufficient funds for his own excavations.

In 1845 he took his spade and milled his way through the middle of the ancient palaces of the vanished empires of Assyria. Of course, he started near the pyramids south of Mosul, which he had come across years before. As soon as he started digging, he found what he was looking for.

He immediately came across palace walls decorated with ivory, cuneiform texts and wonderful pictorial reliefs. Like Botta years before him he was convinced that he had found the real Nineveh. He packed everything into boxes, sent his finds to London, and when he finally returned there eight years after his departure, he was a famous man.

At the end of 1847, he rushed to his new employer, the British Museum. London was by now the greatest city in the world. On display in the bookshops was Robert Chambers' latest book on the 'Vestiges of the Natural History of Creation', an absolute bestseller. All the new scientific discoveries were signs of God's work, the author wrote, hitting the nerve of its readers.

Just a few streets away, Marx and Engels were writing their 'Communist Manifesto', lamenting the miserable conditions of workers in the newly established factories. Three days later, riots were to break out all over Europe. Their book could not have been more topical.

While the continent was engulfed in the turmoils of the 1848 revolutions over the next few months, the young archaeologist sat in front of his desk in London, putting his latest discoveries to paper. His first book, 'Nineveh and Its Remains', was to become an absolute bestseller, it was one of the must-read books at its time. Everyone wanted to know exactly what the ancient biblical kingdoms might have looked like.

However, only short after the publication he had to find out, that he had been as mistaken as Botta was years before him. Layard had discovered ancient Nimrud, as could be proved on some documents he excavated. Ancient Nineveh, however, still remained undiscovered. So what was left for him but to return to Mesopotamia and keep on searching.

Layard's second journey was to bring even more spectacular finds to light. He now drilled tunnels into

'Tell Kujundschik' near Mosul, the beautiful hills where Botta had first tried his hand, before continuing his excavations further north.

This time, in 1849, Layard could be sure that this was ancient Nineveh. What he found was Ashurbanipal's library with thousands of clay tablets. He could be absolutely sure about it simply because it was written on the door. 'Property of Ashurbanipal, King of the World, King of Assyria'. Reading really helps, and you can hardly make it any easier for an archaeologist.

Again, everything was packed into boxes, shipped to London and taken to the British Museum, where all the clay tablets waited to be deciphered over the next few years, including one with the inscription 'K 3375'.

Naked at the museum

When George Smith was born in 1840, Queen Victoria had just ascended her throne and was not to be driven from it for the rest of the century. It was the time when Britain was expanding its empire and becoming an imperial superpower.

George was a typical working-class child of his time with no scientific training. He had started working at the age of fourteen in a print shop not far from the British Museum, and spent every spare minute marvelling at the finds from Mesopotamia. Gradually, he taught himself to decipher cuneiform, and the museum took notice of him.

Eventually, he was offered a job as a restorer, as there were very few people who knew this script at all. His first task was to put together the broken tablets, thousands of which were still lying in the archives waiting to be deciphered. Most of them just contained boring lists of goods or cattle, sometimes a bill of sale, but George was happy and did his job very well.

Years later, after the Prussian king had been proclaimed 'German Emperor' at Versailles, sometime in November of 1872, George was standing in a room on the second floor of the British Museum. Spread out in front of him on a small wooden table were the recently cleaned and partially assembled some of those clay tablets that had been unearthed decades ago in Ashurbanipal's library. Among them was the tablet with the number 'K 3375'.

He was always a little nervous when he got stressed. As he skimmed the first lines, he was already feeling the heat mounting to his head.

'ša nagba īmuru'
he who saw the abyss

George read aloud in a language that had been forgotten for thousands of years. He read of the gods' decision to send a flood to earth to destroy all humans, and of a god named Ea who betrayed the divine plan to the human Utu-napishtim.

Full of excitement, he took off his jacket, opened his collar and rolled up his sleeves. It was certainly a very special tablet, he knew from the beginning. It told a story, and it was the first time for thousands of years it was read out. George focused on the text again again.

God Ea told the man Utu-napishtim to build a large boat for himself and his family, to take birds and animals of all kinds on board.

Like everyone else, George knew his Bible by heart, and the story about a boat looked very familiar. His shirt was soaking wet by now. He took it off and started fiddling with his belt, which began to pinch a little, before he continued reading.

Utu-napishtim obeyed his god Ea, and soon a long rain began. With the rain came a deluge that swallowed all other people and animals from the face of the earth. Then, finally, after seven days, the boat ran aground on a mountain.

George had torrents of sweat running down his forehead when he took of his shoes. The story was almost word by word the same as the one he knew from the Bible. He already knew how it would continue.

Utu-napishtim lets two birds fly that cannot find land, only the last bird, a raven, finally finds a dry shore. Utu-napishtim had survived the deluge together with his family.

'*I am the first person to read this in over two thousand years*,' George shouted out loud as he finally looked up from the text in front of him, his arms wide spread in victory - and almost completely naked.

Important discoveries, it seems, provoke somewhat strange physical reactions at times. Around the time that Georg Grotefend deciphered the first part of the cuneiform script, Jean-Joseph Champollion took his little brother Jean-François by the hand and put him in school with Abbé Dussert, an incident that must have provoked a kind of initial ignition in the brain of the already rather sickly boy.

Within a short time, the twelve-year-old learned not only Greek and Latin, but also Hebrew, Syriac, Arabic, Sanskrit, Persian and later several other languages. There are said to have been around ten in all. Finally, he took the 'Rosetta Stone', which Napoleon had brought back from his Egyptian campaign, and set about deciphering the hieroglyphs.

In September 1822, Jean-François Champollion, as the story goes, ran across the Rue Mazarine in Paris to the library of the 'Institut des Inscriptions' where his brother was working. '*Je tiens l'affaire, je tiens l'affaire*' - I solved it, I solved it, he roared out, wildly gesticulating with his arms in the air. Once again and due to the overwhelming excitement, the young man forgot to breathe, fainted while still running, hit the pavement and spent the next five days in a coma.

Perhaps George had to think of this very incident when he asked himself how such an old story had made it into the Bible. It was about time to take a deep breath and focus on the essentials again, and for George that meant first of all pulling his trousers back up.

The rest of the story is quickly told. The sensation surrounding the discovery of the Flood tablet gripped the entire Christian world, and can perhaps only be compared to the landing of Martians on planet earth today. It was a mixture of fascination and horror.

Over the last few centuries people were rock--solidly convinced that the stories in the Bible were true. All the discoveries in Egypt and Mesopotamia seemed to underline this believe, all the excavations and evidence seemed to speak for the Bible, and now it turned out that the very story of the Deluge, the beginning of all human history, was nothing but an ancient story from Mesopotamia. For many, this was simply inconceivable and turned their entire world view upside down.

George, of course, immediately received the funds for a new excavation in Nineveh. A short time later he was on his way and actually recovered more tablets of a Flood story that turned out to be even much older than the version he had deciphered in London.

Unlike his namesake Georg Grotefend, George Smith was the right man, at the right time, in the right place. Everything pointed to a brilliant career for the young man. He could have become the Charles Darwin of archaeology. What doomed him, however, was a profane bout of diarrhoea that brought his journey to an abrupt end.

He died in August 1876 in Aleppo, the city where Pietro del Valle had fallen in love with his beautiful Aurora.

The Babel-Bible-Controversy

Smith's discovery was immediately taken up by experts. In the same year, Eberhard Schrader, who following the irony of history had studied in Göttingen, published his book 'The cuneiform inscriptions and the old testament', and remarked in it:

> *'The time has probably come when one should take the sickle in one's hand and collect the harvest ripe for cutting. Our previous views of the course of the history of the Orient in the pre-Achaemenid period have been modified in many ways, in some cases reversed from the top to the bottom.*
> *A series of quite unexpected results have presented themselves to the researcher. It is*

understandable that the lion's share of these discoveries falls to the Old Testament; an exploitation of the results of cuneiform decipherment for the same has to begin'.

For many, these lines were incredible and equivalent to the end of the world, and many others still steadfastly clung to a world view and defended an ancient story that had just been disproved.

Let's go back to Berlin and listen to a young professor giving a lecture at the Sing-Akademie in January 1902. His Majesty, Emperor Wilhelm II, was present with his court when Friedrich Delitzsch, so the professor's name, gave his colourfully illustrated lecture on the Mesopotamian epics and the Bible.

Drawing on the new findings of George Smith and many other scholars who had meanwhile studied the subject, Delitzsch explained the origin of the Flood story. He did this in such an impressive way that his audience sat almost paralysed and listened excitedly. It was probably only now that his listeners started to realize that their entire world view had just been laid to rest. He began his lecture this way:

'*Now that the pyramids have opened and the Assyrian palaces have risen, the people of Israel and their writings appear as the youngest of neighbours. A fresh and invigorating wind from the East, coupled with an abundance of light, blows through and illuminates the whole venerable book, and all the more in-*

tensely because Hebrew antiquity is chained from beginning to end precisely with Babylonia and Assyria'.

He told his audience about the roots of the Flood story and its Mesopotamian origin, about the ancient epics, and where they were to be found in the Bible, and of angels, which were actually an invention of much older cultures.

Finally, he pointed out that the Bible is not God's word, but a compilation of various stories gathered and written down by humans. The whole Old Testament ethics and world view went back to the culture of Babylon, he explained, just dismantling the fundamental beliefs of his audience.

While some shocked attendees were still gasping for breath, an elderly, very excited lady made her way through the crowd. Finally arriving in front of the professor, she unleashed a tirade of such savage abuse on him, waving her walking stick so vigorously in front of his nose that the young professor flinched back against the wall, white as a sheet, and refrained from any argument.

The emperor watched the scene and smiled with satisfaction. He seemed to have enjoyed the lecture so much that he had it officially published in the 'Amtlicher Deutscher Reichsanzeiger'. The reactions were tremendous. Church representatives and several Jewish communities went on the barricades, insulted the completely stunned professor in the strongest terms and showered him with abuse and insults. The reaction was so extreme that even the emperor felt compelled to disapprove of Delitzsch's views. It simply could not be what was not allowed to be.

All this was not enough. In the meantime, the lecture had been translated into English and triggered a storm of international indignation. Delitzsch felt compelled to respond to his critics with a second lecture, and after even stronger hostility, with a third lecture.

Finally, one day, a cleric visited him in the Berlin Museum. He gave the professor a sermon with eyes filled with tears, which Delitzsch had to listen to very patiently. '*But, Father,*' he finally asked the still whimpering old man, '*have you read my lectures at all?*' The old man answered in a still trembling voice: '*No, I haven't, but I know what you want to say*'.

For the young Professor that was more than enough. He got his belongings and fled to England to find some distance and a little peace, at least for a while. According to his own information, his luggage contained one thousand three hundred fifty smaller and three hundred larger newspaper and magazine articles, plus sacks of letters 'from Calcutta to the last farm on the California prairie'.

Today, such a reaction is difficult to understand. The Gilgamesh epic has almost been forgotten again, and with it the many stories associated with it. When George Smith translated the Flood story in November 1872, he drove the final nail in the coffin of a completely outdated and long disproved world view that had been firmly entrenched in the minds of society for centuries.

Religion was the foundation of the societies of that time, and one cannot understand the whole of history without repeatedly referring to the role of it. One would think that lessons had finally been learned from the past, but it turns out that it always depends on which story one believes.

For us it's time to go back to the origins to see where some of these stories came from. We have to travel to the place where it all began. It's going to be a long journey through space and time to ancient Mesopotamia. For that you don't get bored on the way, I'll tell you the story of the thirty fertile women from whom we all descend...

Stories about Gilgamesh

The story of the thirty fertile women
Discworld
The stories of Sîn-lēqi-unninni
Sea Peoples with colander
Stories about myths

The story of the thirty fertile women

For most of the human history, land was never scarce and wars were rarely about conquering territory. There was always enough land, what was missing was the population to go with it, and thus taxpayers and potential soldiers. Even in ancient Mesopotamia, there was no lack of fertile land between the Euphrates and the Tigris, but rather of people to cultivate the fields. There were always too few people. Time and again we hear of major resettlement campaigns, both in the Bible and in the cuneiform writings of the Assyrians. Little changed in this 'population problem' until well into the eighteenth century of our time. Let's do a little statistics. Don't worry, it does not hurt and is quite entertaining.

Until about three hundred years ago, you could expect that, statistically, six out of ten people died before the age of fifteen. That was sad, but apparently a law of nature. Hunger, disease, epidemics and natural disasters took a heavy toll. There were always ups and downs, of course, but we are talking about statistics. There was absolutely no question of an overpopulation at all. To illustrate the problem, it is worthwhile to take a small example.

Let's take a small town with two hundred inhabitants, one hundred males and one hundred females of all ages. Of the hundred women, sixty die before they can reproduce, statistically speaking. Of the remaining forty women, some are or become infertile, die in childbirth, enter a convent, are too old or otherwise fail to 'produce' children. Statistically, this leaves about thirty women who have to provide the necessary offspring.

In order to maintain the small village, these thirty women must therefore produce two hundred children, which is about seven children for each woman. In order to be able to provide for a real population growth, these thirty women together must bring at least five more children into the world, because three of them will die before they can reproduce. Statistically, they would have to produce even more children to guarantee, that at least one additional female offspring can continue to reproduce, but let's just leave it at that.

So the number of women has always been decisive, men could largely be dispensed with, as we can already see in the Bible. '*Now therefore, kill every male among the little ones, and kill every woman who has known man by lying with him. But all the young girls who have not known man by lying with him keep alive for yourselves.*' (Numbers 31:17-18). Virgins are spared for the bed, everyone else is slaughtered. But we'd better leave that subject where it is.

So far, so good. Let's calculate what this meant for the lives of the respective women. Statistically, a young couple needs about five months for the first successful pregnancy. This is followed by the usual nine months, and the subsequent breastfeeding period of several months again reduces the probability of becoming pregnant again. A woman can thus, statistically, give birth to a child every 18 months, which adds up to a good eleven years with seven children. But it goes even further. Let's assume that young women are married right at the beginning of their fertile years, which was not unusual until recent times. Then it follows that all women between the ages of sixteen and twenty-eight are either pregnant or busy with breast-feeding their babies.

Now take into account that the man has to feed the family. But only can do so when the father had died and he could finally take over his inheritance. This 'inheritance law' was still quite actual until a few decades ago. However, by then the man was already around thirty, because the father did not intend to die voluntarily before this age. After all, once you had left the childhood diseases behind, you had a good chance of living a little longer.

When the son finally got his inheritance at about thirty, the not-more-so-young man took, of course, had to take a young wife of fifteen years age, and for the next twelve years, this couple was heavily engaged in child production. Sadly, most of their children would die early. The fact that older men take young wives therefore had its origins here and is not particularly disreputable to this day.

All those men who had to wait until they were in their thirties, however, encountered a certain problem, of course. In the prime of their youth, they had to wait for the old man to die until they could finally get going. So the only option available to them was 'extramarital' contact, and that usually meant prostitution.

Alternatively, there was also the possibility of earning enough money through military service, for example, to start a family of their own. And so a little statistics opens up a whole new world. The issue of sex and prostitution has probably been omnipresent in all societies, from ancient times to the present day. So we are all descended from those copulating thirty women, hopefully happily fruiting away, who tried so hard to keep their little village alive.

But let us have a look at what happened in more recent times. With the beginning of the Enlightenment, there was a veritable population explosion and a dramatic demographic change. The population of Europe quadrupled in a short time. The birth rate remained high, average life expectancy increased and infant mortality decreased rapidly. The seemingly natural balance that had existed for hundreds and thousands of years was broken. Suddenly it was no longer only in 'God's hands' whether one survived childhood or was carried off by epidemics or diseases. Slowly, people began to realise that they could have a perspective and a fairly long life ahead of them.

However, as the population grew, living conditions did not automatically improve accordingly. Until then, a high population had been synonymous with growing prosperity of the family and society, but now supply problems, social unrest and economic impoverishment began. Adam Smith had already noticed the many pretty children who flocked around the soldiers' barracks, but rarely reached the age of fifteen. In his 1776 book on the 'Wealth of Nations', he pointed out that in a '*civilised society it is only among the inferior ranks of people that the scantiness of subsistence can set limits to the further multiplication of the human species; and it can do so in no other way than by destroying a great part of the children which their fruitful marriages produce*'.

Thomas Malthus assumed, at the end of the French Revolution in 1798, in his 'Essay on the Principle of Population', that '*in all societies, even those that are most vicious, the tendency to a virtuous attachment is so strong that there is a constant effort towards an increase of population*'.

Food production could not keep pace with population growth in the long run and he predicted that population has a tendency to multiply beyond the measure of available food.

Mathus warned about the coming overpopulation, stating that '*the power of population is so superior to the power in the earth to produce subsistence for man, that premature death must in some shape or other visit the human race*'.

He strongly called for measures to control population growth and warned that 'epidemics, pestilence, and plague, advance in terrific array, and sweep off their thousands and ten thousands. Should success be still incomplete, gigantic inevitable famine stalks in the rear, and with one mighty blow levels the population with the food of the world'. He could not have been more wrong, as we see today.

What happened next no one had foreseen. Contrary to all previous experience, people suddenly stopped reproducing. Where before it had been common to bring eight to ten children into the world, the birth rate dropped drastically to only three or four. This process began in France, the richest and most prosperous country in Europe at the time, and this trend took hold in the other European countries with a time lag.

The wife of the American president, Abigail Adams, complained during her stay in Paris in 1782 about the feeble-minded soft spot of the French for her family, who suddenly only fathered three to four children. At the same time, the Habsburg Maria Theresa still had sixteen offspring, the Prussian soldier king fourteen, and George II of England, who had founded Göttingen University, had 'only' eight children.

The individual factors that led to this sudden 'production stop' within just one century are still not sufficiently clear. Prosperity, education, life expectancy, whatever parameters you apply, they are not sufficient to explain this development. There is only a clue that explains 'why' these ideas took hold in the countries of Europe at such different times. The language.

The new ideas came from France and spread in French. And so it happened that the ideas spread much earlier in the French-speaking south of Belgium than in the Flemish-speaking north. The same was observed in Spain, where the ideas began to take hold at different times in the individual language regions.

Of course, you need a common language to be able to exchange ideas and tell stories. But that something as mundane as 'common language' could have such an impact astonished even the researchers from Princeton, who tackled this issue in the 1970s with the 'Princeton Fertility Project'.

But unfortunately we have to stop here, because after this long journey through space and time we have finally reached the destination of our journey, the place where it all began. Welcome to Uruk!

Discworld

The world of Sîn-lēqi-unninni was round. It was about as round as one of the first known maps in history, found in one of the many excavations in Mesopotamia. The world was round, surrounded by water with Mesopotamia at its centre and the Euphrates running through it. It shows the Persian Gulf to the south and indicates cities or peoples in the inner circle.

Whether one can claim that the people of Mesopotamia saw the world as a disc because of the map, however, may be doubted. In fact, no one able to calculate properly believed in it, and they were pretty good at it in Uruk. Nevertheless, many people still believe that even in the Middle Ages people were convinced that the world was a disc.

It was probably Antoine-Jean Letronne, professor at the highly respected Collège de France in Paris and an expert on the history of Egypt, who started this nonsense. In 1838, Letronne was dealing with the question of what image the ancients had of the world. He was not yet familiar with the Epic of Gilgamesh, but like some of his colleagues, he opposed the backwardness of the Catholic Church.

That same year he published his book 'Des Opinions cosmographiques des Pères de l'Église' - On the cosmological opinions of the church fathers, in which he accused them of taking the Bible too literally: '*La terre plate, le ciel formant une vòute solide au-dessous de laquelle est la couche des eaux célestes, voilà les notions fondamentales de la cosmographie biblique*' - a flat earth, with a dome above, some clouds on it and that's it with cosmic fundamentals of the Bible', he berated the clergy. The Church has held this view throughout the Middle Ages, he said, opposing the progress of true philosophy and scientific observation.

'*They persecute Galileo, fear Descartes, and represent a world view that is even older than the Ptolemaic one*', Letronne accused the church representatives. Rather, the papal theologians condemn the new findings as philosophically absurd and as religious heresy. He really did pull them to pieces, and his views were only too readily taken up and forwarded by others. Shortly after the first newspaper articles appeared and a new myth was born. What has survived to this day is above all the view that the Church held until the dark Middle Ages that the Earth was a disc.

It is said that even today there are people who seriously believe in the disc shape of the world. However, the only really existing disc world can be found in the novels of the fantasy author Terry Pratchett, who also answers the question of whether the back of this disc is inhabited. According to him, the discworld rests on four giant elephants that drift through space on the back of the galactic turtle A-Tuin.

But where there are people who believe in a flat earth, there are also people who believe in the Flying Spaghetti Monster and wear a noodle strainer on their heads. You might laugh, but it really exists, this community of believers.

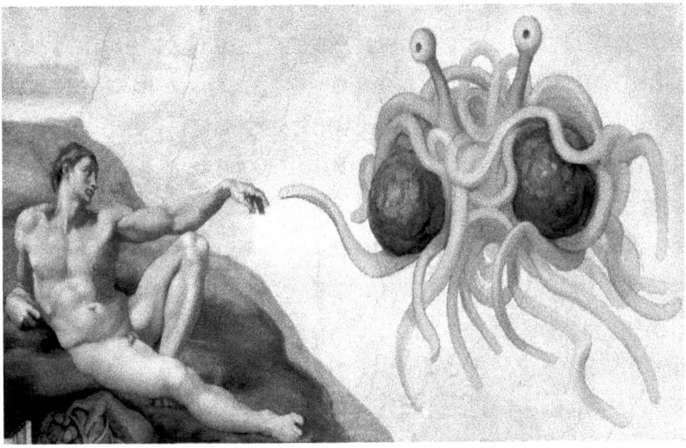

The stories of Sîn-lēqi-unninni

But let us now have a closer look to Uruk, where they are busy preparing for a great festival. On the large square in front of the temple, the first beer booths are being set up, and right next to them they the barbecues for the many animals sacrificed are being prepared. Beer, barbecue, the only thing missing seem to be French fries, but America had not been discovered yet. So let's take a seat and have a cool drink, just what we need after the long journey. They do really have beer here, no joke! Come on, I invite you. And then we listen to the story of Sîn-lēqi-unninni. He's sitting over there.

Sîn-lēqi-unninni, which means something like 'the moon god hears my prayers', was still sitting in front of his small desk in a temple. Uruk was the city where it all began, the first thriving metropolis on both sides of the Euphrates River, which was running right through it. It was a beautiful city, with monumental buildings and colourful statues of Ishtar, the goddess of love. The huge palaces were painted blue and large colourful temples in honour of god Maduk were all over. Uruk already had a long history, so long that it stretched back to the beginning, and Sîn-lēqi-unninni was well aware of it.

The city was surrounded by a huge fortress wall, more than eleven kilometres long, which the ancient king Gilgamesh had built ages ago. It was the largest city in the world, and no one could compete with it. Fifty thousand people lived here, with many other settlements surrounding the town. The palace and the temples organised the city. Building orders had to be placed, the fields ploughed and irrigation prepared. The dams and pipes were maintained and cultivation organised.

Large herds of goats and sheep also belonged to the temples. In addition, there was the administration of justice and the courts, the issuing of deeds, the distribution of land ownership, the many workshops for the production of the most exquisite goods, and of course trade, which extended far in all directions and reached into the most remote countries.

Uruk was a cosmopolitan city, the city of Sîn-lēqi-unninnis was the seat of government and the political and economic centre. Here there was mathematics, medicine, philosophy, in short, Uruk was the centre of the world, at least for the priest and his family.

It was early afternoon in 1177 BC and it had already become pleasantly cool. Sîn-lēqi-unninni was a scribe, but not alone for the palace or the temple. After months of hard work he had completed his own monumental work. And just now he pressed his name into a corner of the clay tablet before giving it to burn so that it would harden.

In front of him lay the last of a total of twelve clay tablets on which he had finished his writing. He had created a beautiful epic and was sure that it would make him immortal. In the weeks and months before, he had selected the most beautiful stories that were told and bend them together in one overwhelming epic. Certainly the story of the creation of the world, Enuma Elis, could not be missing.

> '*E-nu-ma e-liš la na-bu-ú šâ-ma-mu - when on high the heaven had not been named, and firm ground below had not been called by name*', began this epic in his language.
> '*When even Apsu, the primordial river-god, the begetter of the gods, and Mummu Tiâmat, the sea-goddess, who bore them all, mingled their waters into one, when no reed hut had been matted, no marsh land had appeared, when no god had yet appeared, uncalled by name, their destinies undetermined, then it was when the gods were formed from the womb of Apsu and Tiâmat*'.

The epic was about a terrible battle between the new gods. As more and more were born, it had become noisy, and their noise disturbed the peace of the creator of gods. Apsu therefore decided to kill them all, the children's behaviour was unbearable.

> '*During the day I cannot rest, at night I cannot sleep. I want to destroy them to put an end to their doings. Silence shall reign so that we can sleep*', said Apsu, the river god.

But Tiamat, the sea goddess who gave birth to them all, refused. The god Ea finally killed Apsu. Other gods convinced Tiamat to avenge his death. Terrible monsters were created and cruel wars waged. Finally, the great Marduk, designated by the other gods as their leader, won the battle against the sea goddess Tiamat. And Marduk cut open Tiamat's body and formed the heavens and the earth from it:

> *'So he cut it in two like a dried fish and used one half to make the vault of heaven... He heaped fertile mounds on its breast. He drilled a water table to make a spring. From a loop of her tail he created the bond of heaven and earth'.*

Marduck created time and determined the course of the moon and stars. He divided the gods as rulers of the heavens and the underworld, and they built the city of Babylon as his sanctuary in gratitude. And from the blood of Tiamat's husband Kingu, he finally created humans, so that they might bear the toil of the gods and the gods might thereby have their rest:

> *'A tissue of blood will I make, bones will I form, to make a being come into being. Adam be his name'.*

These were the great epics that have been told since time immemorial. And of course, the story of Atrahasis, the extraordinarily wise king of Shuruppack, which the old Nur-Aya had so wonderfully compiled long ago, was not to be missed. In this epic, the gods complained about the hard work they had. Man should do the work of the gods, they demanded, and the wise god Enki decided on the creation of man and said:

> *'Nintu shall dress the clay with his flesh and his blood. Thus God and man mingle in the clay'.*

Finally, Ma'ami, the mother goddess, created man from clay and the blood of the god Geshtu-e, a god with intellect.

> *'Seven parts clay for man, seven parts clay for woman.... Woman and man shall find each other, seven days shall the love feast of Ishtar last and the woman shall give birth in the tenth month'.*

But people reproduced too much and again disturbed the peace of the supreme god Enlil. '*The noise of the people is too much, their noise disturbs my sleep*' he said, and sent diseases and pestilences to the earth to decimate the people. But again and again the god Enki appeared and warned the wise Atrahasis, and again and again the people survived the gods' attempts to wipe them from the earth.

Finally Enlil decided to send a deluge, and again the wise Atrahasis was warned by Enki. He received precise instructions to build a boat to save himself, his family and all the animal species. The gods sent a storm, after seven days the flood ended, and the boat landed on a mountain. The gods themselves had become weak, because they were feeding on the sacrifices of men. So they allowed the wise Atrahasis, king of Shuruppack, to live on, and they gave him immortality.

For weeks, Sîn-lēqi-unninni had read the ancient scriptures, including the stories of Humbaba, a giant monster that guards Inanna's cedar forests in the north. And the many stories about the goddess of love Ishtar, for example, when she descends into the underworld. At each of the seven gates she passed through, she had to remove a piece of clothing. Finally, she reached her destination completely unclothed and died. But with that, there was no more love, growth, fruit or offspring in the world. Only by trickery was she saved, and only in this way did life return to the world.

There were beautiful stories circulating in the world of Sîn-lēqi-unninni, and he had to sort out many of them. Such was the story of the goddess Inanna and Schu-kale-tuda, her gardener. Schu-kale-tuda saw Inanna, the erotic goddess of love, sleeping under a shady tree in the paradisical garden. The goddess was so irresistible that Shu-kale-tuda could not control himself and raped her in her sleep.

Only when Inanna awoke did she realise what had been done to her. She searched for the villain in all the hidden corners of the world, transformed herself into a rainbow and spied the culprit in his hiding place under a bush. In vain the scamp begged for his life, but the goddess promised, that his story should be told for all time. Then she killed him, for no man raped a goddess with impunity.

It had become a mighty epic that laid before Sîn-lēqi-unninni, 'ša nagba īmuru' - he who saw the abyss, that was how his work was to begin. He had finished it just in time for the upcoming festival in Uruk, where the work was to be publicly recited. His version and the way in which he wove the most diverse stories together was certainly worthy of this year's winner's prize.

His epic simply had everything it needed: adventurous journeys to the end of the world, angry gods, daring heroes battling giants, and of course a good dose of sex. And yet it was also a profound story about living, dying and the origin of man.

The hero of the story was Gilgamesh, king of Uruk. He was two parts god, and one part man. And he was a disgusting martinet, this Gilgamesh, who behaved like a rutting bull in a pen of sheep. He made the men slave away until they dropped, building the city wall or working in the fields, so that even the whores of the city complained about the lack of customers. And while the men were too exhausted to lie with their wives, Gilgamesh pursued every virgin, every bride, and every woman in his city, and mounted every woman that was not up in the trees in time.

Finally, the gods took pity on the pleas of the citizens and sent Enkidu, a being two parts a man, one part an animal. To civilise him, he was sent the harlot Shamhat, who had wild sex with him for six days and seven nights. After Enkidu had also learned to eat and drink, he finally met Gilgamesh in battle. But neither could defeat the other, and so they became friends and set off together on adventurous journeys through the world of that time.

They defeated the giant Humbaba, who guarded the cedar fields of Lebanon, and robbed his treasures. They insulted Ishtar, the goddess of love, and in the end, Enkidu had to die for his many crimes. Gilgamesh mourned at the side of his stinking and decaying carcass until the maggots fell out of his nose.

In despair and in search of immortality, he met Utu-napishtim and his wife, the only survivors of the deluge, which lasted six days and seven nights. When Gilgamesh was asked to prove his willpower by giving up sleep for six days and seven nights, he immediately fell asleep for six days and seven nights. Finally, a herb given to him as a parting gift, promising at least eternal youth, was eaten by a snake. Thus humbled and purified, Gilgamesh returned home to Uruk and finally surrendered to his mortal fate.

If this was not the most wonderful story, thought Sîn-lēqi-unninni, then the world should come to an end. The preparations for the feast in the temple were almost complete. Huge quantities of bread were made, dozens of sheep and goats were washed and cleaned. The feast was to last ten days, and the city was to have enough to eat and to drink. People were to praise Ishtar, and some young people already started celebrating, singing Ishtar's songs along with the young women who were waiting for them:

'Since I'm ready to give you all what you want, get all the young men of your city together, let's go to the shade of the wall.
Seven for her midriff, seven for her loins, sixty then sixty satisfy themselves in turn upon her nakedness.
The young men have tired, Ishtar never tires.
Put it on my lovely vulva, fellows!
As the girl demanded the young men heeded, gave her what she asked for'

Shamhat and her colleagues would have a long night ahead, that was for sure. Later, his story would also be recited in the great square. This evening was to do all honour to Sîn-lēqi-unninni and his epic.

'ša nagba īmuru' - who saw the abyss, was how his work began, and that is exactly what was to happen. Sîn-lēqi-unninni was really looking deep into the abyss, because tonight, in 1177 BC, the world was going to end, and with it the entire civilisation was going to collapse. What had happened?

Sea Peoples with colander

Until a few years ago, the story of the Sîn-lēqi-unninni would have continued as follows: In the year 1177, about six thirty in the evening, the wild hordes of the 'Sea Peoples' suddenly appeared at the city gates. Some of these wild fellows wore colourful tufts of feathers on their heads, others helmets with long horns placed on them, and once or twice a colander is said to have been spotted.

These wild hordes robbed, murdered, pillaged and raped everything and everyone they could get their hands on. They came by the thousands, by countless ships from the west across the sea, and overland in a vast troop of never-ending murdering masses. The stream of these wild barbarians set itself in motion another incredible migration of peoples.

They scaled the walls of all the rich and prosperous cities that lay in their path. Greek Mycenae fell, as did Troy of Priam. The empire of the Hittites perished, their fleet destroyed Crete and burned down the rich cities of the Levant. An entire age fell victim to this onslaught of the 'Sea Peoples'. It was the end of the 'Bronze Age'.

Only Egypt was able to resist this unruly storm, and in a last decisive battle, Ramses III fought the hordes at the gates of his empire before the world could come to rest again. '*A last alliance of men and elves marched against the armies of Mordor. And on the slopes of Mount Doom they fought for the freedom of Middle Earth*'.

Should now dwarves and hobbits appear on the scene, one is inevitably reminded of Tolkien's 'Lord of the Rings'. Obviously, something had gone totally wrong with this story of these 'Sea Peoples'. So let's have a look, since when this story is being told and how it developed over time.

But first things first. The date 1177 BC results from the book title of historian Eric Cline, '1177 BC: The

First Fall of Civilisation', a historian who, like many of his colleagues, is still puzzling over how the 'Bronze Age' could have come to an end. That it is merely a fictional story is disregarded. But let's just ask ourselves how long we have been telling ourselves this story.

The whole story about the 'Sea Peoples' started around 1855 with Emmanuel de Rougé, the later head of the College de France. The Egyptologist referred to a depiction on a relief that could be dated to 1179 B.C., the time of Ramses III. The inscription on the depiction spoke of 'attackers from the north', there was no mentioning of 'sea peoples', not at all.

Mr Champollion, who was in a coma for five days after deciphering the hieroglyphs, had already made some suggestions about the origin of the people depicted on the relief. To this, de Rougé added that '*les Schartana et les Tonirasch portent la désignation de 'peuples de la mer'* - that the Schartana and the Tonirasch bore the designation 'peoples of the sea', and that they could therefore possibly have come from the islands or coasts of the archipelago. It was pure speculation and the birth of the 'Sea Peoples Myth'. From now on, everyone imagined their own story about the origin of these 'Sea Peoples'.

For Gaston Maspero, his successor at the Collège de France, the story had already reached biblical proportions. For him, the story already began in Western Europe, with 'great European masses' supposedly setting off for the Balkans for whatever reason. There they drove out the inhabitants who, on the one hand, left for Greece, now driving out the Greeks themselves, who in turn founded new cities in Asia Minor and elsewhere in the Mediterranean. On the other hand, the Balkan inhabitants are also said to have come across the Bosporus, triggering a huge migration movement there. In his book '*The Struggle of Nations', published* 1896, he describes the first mass migration in history like this:

> *'The peoples who originally lived in these regions now found themselves fleeing from the invading hordes, and were forced to take every conceivable route to the south and east'*

When Eduard Meyer, one of the most important German historians of his time, finally published his mammoth work 'Geschichte des Alterthums' (History of Antiquity) a few years later, in 1913, the view that the 'Sea Peoples' from the West were responsible for the downfall of the former civilisations in the East had already gained acceptance.

According to him, the whole world had conspired against Egypt, for now even the Libyans allied with the 'Sea Peoples' and launched a large, carefully prepared attack on Egypt.

> The '*invasion of Egypt is part of a great movement of peoples which has shaken and largely reshaped the entire eastern basin of the Mediterranean together with the adjacent mainland*', he wrote in his five-volume work.

The success of the 'Sea Peoples' myth had a very simple reason. Like Tolkien's book 'The Lord of the Rings', it had all the elements of a great story, and was unbeatably simple. The term 'Bronze Age' had only been invented a few years ago. Also, many people thought to be at the verge of a new era at this time, and with the relief from Egypt they invented a story that fitted wonderfully into the late nineteenth-century Europe.

The first problem, however, is that three thousand years ago there simply were no 'masses' of people in Western Europe who could possibly have wandered off. Europe was still quite empty that time. There was enough land, only the population was lacking. Our thirty fertile women could have tried as much as they wanted, but they would never ever had been able to produce a population explosion. The issue of 'over-population' only came up in the late eighteenth century with Thomas Malthus, and when Meyer wrote his work, Europe had indeed become more crowded.

It was, secondly, the time when the great European powers began to divide up the world among themselves. The age of imperialism had just begun, colonies seemed to be vital for the survival of the nwely formed 'nations', and the conquest of new territories was understood as a 'struggle for existence'. In addition, a rather unhealthy nationalism was just spreading, the Franco-German war had only recently ended and the Prussian king had been appointed as 'German Emperor'.

'History' as a discipline had just been invented, and more and more analogies were being made between the antiquity and the present. Meyer, together with many other German scholars, was of the opinion that '*without German militarism (...) German culture would have long since been wiped off the face of the earth*'.

People were racing full steam ahead towards the world wars of the twentieth century. It was a warlike time in which Meyer and his colleagues developed the 'Sea Peoples Myth'.

As you might know, you always find exactly what you are looking for, or rather, you only ever look for exactly what you want to find. It is somewhat reminiscent of the story of that slightly drunk man who is looking for his keys one night under the light of a street light. A second man comes along, asks if he can help, and together they search the illuminated area under the lantern. After a while, the second man begins to have doubts and asks the first man, if he is sure that he has lost his keys here. '*No*', he replies, '*I lost them over there, but there is no light there*'.

It is still similar today, and people often interpret events on the basis of their own experiences. People are only too happy to search in the cone of light of the street lamp and easily fall into patterns of interpretation that they are already familiar with.

When the societies in Eastern Europe and the Soviet Union collapsed a few decades ago, for example, people looked for clues as to whether the demise of the 'Bronze Age' might not have had similar causes. Of course evidence was found to support this assumption.

When the topic of 'climate change' came to the attention of researchers, they, of course, found climatic changes in some areas in the Mediterranean. Today, people believe in 'globalisation', and you may imagine what reasons are now being blamed. The trade and production chains were so complex back then that the whole system collapsed when just one link in the chain was destroyed. Among all the ancient clay tablets from Mesopotamia there was indeed a letter from the city of Mari that refers to this phenomenon in an astonishing way. It reports the return of a pair of Minoan-style leather shoes that had previously been delivered to the court of Hamurapi in Babylon. However, the letter does not indicate whether shape, colour or size of the shoes delivered were responsible for the cancellation of the order, but the parallels with today are simply ingenious.

All this, of course, proves absolutly nothing. Riots happen all the time, environmental changes happen everywhere, and you can always buy new shoes.

Most likely, nothing extraordinary happened. Changes can happen in three hundred years, but the myth of the 'Sea Peoples' is still a very nice story. And it is very likely, that it will soon be proven that a pandemic ended the Bronze Age, just wait and see.

Stories about myths

It is always exciting to observe who uses which myth at what time and for what purpose. Most of the time, myths tell little or nothing about historical truths, but about beautiful stories which one can identify with. Some of these myths define a common enemy, others tell of alliances, and they are always meant to incite common thinking and action. They exist in all cultures, at all times, and on all topics, and they can always adapt to the current situation.

The myth of 'globalisation', for example, is a multifunctional myth that is now blamed for everything. It emerged around 1995 and initially described nothing more than the international movement of goods between countries and different regions of the world, as it had existed long before. But now it is also responsible for bad weather, the 'burn-out' syndrome and cough. In itself it is complete nonsense and has nothing to do with the original term, but as with the story of the 'Sea Peoples', it is so beautiful that many cling to this myth and keep adding new elements.

Other myths stem from the time when the first nation states were created and a 'national identity' and common history had to be invented. When the statue of Vercingetorix was inaugurated in France in 1865, the history of France suddenly reached back to the Gauls. '*A united Gaul, forming one nation, inspired by the same spirit, can defy all*' is inscribed on the oversized monument in Alise-Sainte-Reine, the presumed site of the battle against the Romans in Julius Caesar's time. This also created a common image of the enemy against the Prussians, who were to pass by in a few years.

Shortly after the Prussian king was proclaimed 'German Emperor' in Versailles, a 'German' past was needed. Only now the 'German' Middle Ages were invented, and in the national exuberance Richard Wagner wrote his 'Ring of the Nibelungs'. When the Hermann Monument was erected in Detmold in 1875, this 'German' history suddenly stretched back to the ancient Germanic tribes, according to the monuments inscriptions: '*He who unites long-divided tribes with a strong hand, who victoriously overcomes Roman power and treachery, who leads long-lost sons home to the German Empire, Armin, he is our saviour*'

When the wave of nationalism swept into Spain at

the beginning of the 19th century - shortly after the French Revolution - there was suddenly talk of the 'Reconquista', a term that only appeared for the first time around 1796, some three hundred years the Moors were driven out of the peninsula. The only question that remains is, what was actually being 're-conquered', since 800 years earlier there had been no 'Spain' at all. However, to this day, this term is used to strengthen Spanish national sentiment.

Such founding myths have been known since antiquity. Even today, for example, many textbooks contain the story of the 'Ionian migration', in which the first settlers came from mainland Greece and were driven out by the 'hordes from the west', most likely the 'Sea Peoples'. In antiquity, however, there were roughly four different groups of foundation myths of the Ionian cities, many existing in parallel, and some completely contradicting each other.

Some cities cited Athens as their city of origin, some the Aegean region in general. A smaller proportion also referred to Phoenicia and the Near East, and many foundation myths were local in nature. Sometimes it seemed appropriate to come from Athens, sometimes from Troy, sometimes from Tyros. It was never a matter of historical fact, but of a good story with which people could and should identified.

The city of Smyrna, for example, traced its history back to the Amazons, who were allied with Troy; to the Aiolians, when the city had concluded a trade agreement with eleven other 'Aiolian' cities; to the Ionians, when the 'Ionian League' was agreed between twelve cities; to Theseus, who went with Heracles against the Amazons; to Pelops from Asia Minor, who was cut into pieces by his father Tantalus and presented to the gods for a meal; and, finally, to a few others who went back to the ancient Assyrians.

Even the Bible and Homer's Iliad are bursting with foundation myths and family stories that seem to go back for centuries. Homer's heroes obviously have a god somewhere in their long line of ancestors, and at epic length the warriors before Troy spread out their web of relationships before they finally smash each other's skulls in.

In the Bible, famous founding father Abraham comes from Mesopotamia, where Noah survived the deluge. Or the population comes from Egypt, from where Moses came and where people always fled when food became scarce. Two founding myths in the same story, and nobody had a problem with that.

To this day, people seem to be obsessed with knowing where someone comes from. It defines who you are, gives information about your character, and determines your relationship to each other and towards others. It's actually complete nonsense, and most of the time they are made-up stories that only last as long as people believe in them.

Let's just hope that the 'Sea Peoples' is just one of those stories, that Sîn-lēqi-unninni didn't have to look into the abyss on his big night and still had an interesting life ahead of him.

Since good stories never die out, it's about time to see where the old myths from Mesopotamia resurface.

We have already seen some parallels with the story of the Flood, and you can find more of them in the Bible. So let's travel through time and take a look at what is written in this bestseller, which very likely only very few people really read very carefully.

On our way to the biblical time, I will tell you something about our alphabet. After all, the holy script was not written in cuneiform, right?

Biblical Stories

Ox-House-Camel

Astruc's knife

Smartphones and Camels

The bride sold

Biblesex

A sheep called 'Daisy'

Ox-House-Camel

There is one thing, however, that certainly took place during the three hundred or so years of the so-called 'Dark Ages'. When written documentation broke down in the eastern Mediterranean region around 1200 BC, a new script emerged somewhere in the Levant to which we owe our present alphabet.

Until then, the writing used independent symbols for terms like 'ox', 'house', 'camel', 'door', i.e. a painted ox, a painted house, a painted camel and a painted door. Now people started to use letters or syllables according to their pronunciation.

The advantage was obvious. Instead of learning thousands of different characters by heart, about twenty-six letters or syllables were now sufficient. Also, there was no longer a need for clay tablets, because writing in clay is almost impossible. Other materials were increasingly used, such as leather, wax and finally papyrus.

To learn the new alphabet, the same method was used as schoolchildren still do it today: A for apple, B for ball, C for chicken and so on. At that time, people learned accordingly: A for Alpu, B for Betu, G for Gamlu, D for Damlu. ABGD - 'alpu', 'betu', gamlu', 'damlu', which resulted in a funny and nonsensical sequence of pictures: ox - house - camel - door.

Soon, the first Greek pupils learned their alpha, beta, gamma and delta, and in a weird way, still today we begin our alphabet with ox-house-camel. Some things just never die out.

Whether the documentation from the old days died out because of the new alphabet and the new writing materials is still unclear, and will probably remain a mystery forever. In any case, the first stories of the Bible were written down shortly after, and Homer's Iliad was written at about the same time. For a long time, these both texts were said to be the oldest existing literary testimonies in the history of Western mankind. Reason enough to take a closer look at both works soon.

However, as revolutionary as the invention of the modern alphabet may seem, it certainly cannot be held responsible as the key to particularly high cultural, literary or scientific achievement. Anyone who claims this should try to learn Japanese. There, two forms of the syllabic script 'hiragana' and 'katagana' are still used in parallel, each with forty-six phonetic syllabic characters. In addition, there are the rather figurative 'kanjis' borrowed from Chinese, of which no one knows how many thousands actually exist. People read from 'left to right' and from 'front to back', as well as from 'top to bottom' and from 'back to front'. The Western alphabet seems mundane even to a Japanese first-grader.

As if that is not enough, the almost infinite possibilities of Japanese numerals are worth considering. The number three is generally translated as 'san' in Japanese. However, a pedantic distinction is made between what is counted and what is not. Thin flat objects (san-mai leaves), slender tall objects (san-bon trees), small animals (san-biki dogs), large animals (san-bo elephants) and birds (san-wa birds). For sweets, -ko is used, for books -satsu, and for ages -sai. There is a name for almost anything and everything, be it machines, floors, small copper or large silver coins. The possibilities seem endless.

Anyone who takes the trouble to learn this language cannot help feeling that it is a diffuse, collective revenge of Japan, designed solely to harass Western 'long-noses' who came so uninvited to their country a few hundred years ago. And in spite of the Japanese language, which seems so extensive and complicated, no one can claim that Japan is in any way culturally, economically or literarily backward, rather the opposite is the case. And above all, they are very nice people indeed.

But now, welcome to the biblical times, and let's turn to the oldest written documents available to our Western civilisation, starting with the Bible.

Astruc's knife

With the discovery of the Epic of Gilgamesh, it became clear that the story of the biblical Flood was only a copy of a much older tale from the Mesopotamian saga. In 1883, Julius Wellhausen caused a worldwide sensation when he put forward the thesis in his 'Prolegomena to the History of Israel' that the first books of Moses were based on four different sources that were included in the Bible centuries after Moses' lifetime. Following the irony of this story, Wellhausen was a professor in Göttingen, and his thesis was long considered a foundational work of biblical criticism, at least until it was discovered that far more sources than the four mentioned were used in Scripture.

A year later, the leading Assyriologist François Lenormant claimed that many stories from the Books of Moses originally came from Mesopotamia, were already told for centuries and passed on from generation to generation. He also points to remarks by the Babylonian priest Bel-re'u-su, or Berossos in Greek, from the third century B.C., who identified the ancient epics as ancient Mesopotamian sagas.

Lenormant and Wellhausen were able to draw on a book by Jean Astruc that had been published more than a hundred years earlier. Astruc had noticed the use of different names, 'Elohim' and 'Jahwe' in the Holy Script. He therefore suspected two different sources of the Genesis and published his findings in 1753 in the book 'Conjectures on the original documents that Moses appears to have used in composing the Book of Genesis. With remarks that support or throw light upon these conjectures'.

Astruc was actually born in Brussels in 1684, but later he was living and working in France. He became an advisor to King Louis XV, and for a short time the lover of Madame de Tencin, who caused a stir in Paris at the time.

This Claudine Guérin de Tencin was something like the 'femme fatal' of the French society of her time. She was called 'La maîtresse publique', intelligent, wealthy, and in many ways far ahead of her time, including her countless lovers. Originally, her parents had destined her to become a nun. Fortunately, she escaped this fate, earned a fortune through speculative trading, became a writer, and had strong political influence on the King of France through one of her lovers, the Maréchal de Richelieu. At one point, she even had to spend some time in the Bastille prison after one of her lovers took his own life out of despair over his lover's faithlessness.

But back to Jean Astruc, whose brief liaison with Madame de Tencin made him a highly respected doctor in Paris, who ironically specialised in the study of sexually transmitted diseases. As an orthodox Catholic, it was actually his intention to defend the 'Holy Scriptures', which were coming under increasing criticism for their long-known contradictions in the first five books of Moses.

Astruc was probably one of the first 'enlighteners', but most likely completely unintentionally. He took his Bible and a piece of paper one day, and wrote on one side all the texts that bore the name Yahweh, and on the other side those texts that called the name Elohim. After he had made some lists, there were two separate stories in front of him, apparently brought together in the Bible. So Moses had used two different stories, he thought.

Even if he did not say it specifically, he was completely unintentionally implying that the stories were not written by Moses. Astruc, therefore, preferred to publish his book in the more liberal Brussels rather than in Catholic Paris. With this discovery, he became the father of modern biblical analysis, although more by accident and quite unintentionally.

'Astruc, King Louis XV's personal physician, first laid knife and probe to the Pentateuch', Goethe wrote about him a few years later. *'And what have not the sciences in general already owed to the participating lovers and unbiased hospitallers!'* True enough! It probably could not be formulated more aptly.

So it's time to take a closer look at the book we've been talking about all this time. Don't worry, there will be no religious instruction, but some of the stories do hold a surprise ... or two...

Smartphones and Camels

Welcome to the biblical times. We are around the year 800 BC, the mysterious 'Sea Peoples' have gone and the world has changed quite a bit. The empires of Mycenae and the Hittites no longer exist, the first Greek city-states make their appearance, and in northern Africa a young girl named Elissa, the daughter of the Tyrian king Mutto, cuts a cowhide into extremely thin strips and uses it to span the land on which the city of Carthage will be founded. In Italy, the abandoned brothers Romulus and Remus are suckled by a wolf, and will soon start a dispute with Aeneas, the fleeing king's son from burning Troy, over who gets to found Rome, the future centre of the western world. Foundation myths never die out.

The use of cuneiform writing is becoming rarer,

and the 'ox-house-camel' ABC we know today is slowly gaining acceptance, the poet Homer writes down his Iliad, and the first stories of the Bible are compiled in the mountainous hinterland of the Levant. Unfortunately, we don't know who wrote the Bible as authors did not indicate their name.

However, there are some hints as to when the stories were compiled, as there are some historical events and the names of various rulers who also appear in other written records in Mesopotamia and Egypt. These include the Egyptian pharaohs Shoshenq and Taharqa, Assyrian kings such as Sanherib or Ashurbanipal, and of course the Babylonian Nebuchadnezzar and the Persian Cyrus. All historically persons, at least as far as we know today.

There are also some traces of the now extinct Hittites in the Bible. They appear when Abraham buys his deceased wife a burial box from them, while the son amuses himself with Rebekah in his dead mother's tent (Genesis 24.67).

They also appear in the story of Esau and Jacob, where Jacob wrests the birthright from his elder brother after a lentil soup. His mother Rebekah insists that Jacob should not take a 'Hittite woman' as wife. So Jacob flees to his maternal uncle in Mesopotamia, falls in love with his younger cousin Rachel, ends up in bed with his older cousin Leah on their wedding night, finally marries both sisters, and also inseminates their maidservants Zilpah and Bilhah.

The twelve children of these four women would later form the twelve tribes of Israel (Genesis 29-30).

There are wonderful stories in the Bible, including foundation myths. Nevertheless, the book was not written at the time of the Hittites, but merely took over the old stories from them, for the scripture is brimming with obvious contradictions. If, for example, Robin Hood suddenly pulls out his smartphone and texts something to his girlfriend Marian, there must be something wrong with this story. And the smartphone of the Bible is the camel.

Camels were not used for caravan transports until about the eighth or seventh century BC; before that, only donkeys were used. Camels simply do not fit into the time of the Hittites. Just as Robin Hood did not have a smartphone, the Hittites did not have camels. And yet, right from the very first stories of the Bible, camels appear as means of transport not just once, but in more than twenty occasions.

'*Then the servant took ten of his master's camels and departed...*' (Genesis 24.10). The camel caravan in the story, in which Joseph is at first in danger of being slain by his brothers, but is then sold to merchants to Egypt also refers to trade routes to Arabia, which themselves did not exist until the Assyrian Empire in the eighth and seventh centuries (Genesis 37.25). There are numerous other hidden references to the time when the various parts of the Bible were written together. So when Robin Hood tweets a message to his girlfriend, it should strike an attentive reader as a little odd.

The Bible is an epic composed of an astonishingly large number of different stories that have been edited, adapted and changed again and again over the centuries. So today it is fairly certain that this process began for the 'Old Testament' around 800 BC, and was completed in 160 BC. Now that we know when the Bible was written, we should take a look at what stories it consists of. One finds ancient Mesopotamian as well as Egyptian myths and legends, and on top of that, some stories are repeated several times.

The bride sold

The unknown authors of the Bible script had the following problems. They first had to decide which stories should be included, and which of their many versions should be told. They also had to rearrange them to fit them into a single story, and last but not least reformulate them in such a way that all was focused on one god only. As always in life when facing just a difficult task, the result was a compromise. So let's have a look what we have got here and start with the old epics from Uruk.

We find the ancient stories of Sîn-lēqi-unninni right in the first sentence of the Bible. '*In the beginning God created the heavens and the earth*'. It is nothing else than a modified form of the epic 'Enuma Elis', in which the god Marduk created heaven and earth.

'*E-nu-ma e-liš la na-bu-ú šâ-ma-mu*' - when on high the heaven had not been named, and firm ground below had not been called by name. That is: 'in the beginning'.

Marduk cut Tiamat's body in two like a dried fish, from one half he created the firmament, from the other the earth, thus: 'created the heavens and earth'.

And now delete Marduk and Tiamat and replace it with one 'God'. There you are, right in the beginning. But there is even more evidence.

In both stories a firmament is created above the earth, in both light is created first, and time afterwards, and again and again the number 'seven' is of great importance. In the Bible it is said after the respective deeds that it was 'good', in the ancient myths that it was 'beautiful'. In both works, the earth and its inhabitants are created from the initial chaotic waters, first the living beings in the water, then those on land.

Man in the Bible is formed from clay, or earth, 'Adamah', and is therefore called Adam, the 'Man'. In the ancient epic 'Atrahasis' it is said, '*Nintu shall dress the clay with his flesh and his blood. Thus God and man mingle in the clay. A tissue of blood will I make, bones will I form, to make a being come into being: Adam be his name*'.

In the ancient epics, the Mother Goddess created man from seven parts of clay for man, and seven parts of clay for woman. In the Bible it says '*So God created man in his own image, in the image of God he created him; male and female he created them*' (Genesis 1.27). So it may well be that God was originally a woman. The 'rib-story' comes later.

There were several versions of the story of the deluge in Mesopotamia. In the Atrahasis epic, the king of Shuruppack builds a ship and thus survives the

Flood. When Sîn-lēqi-unninni wrote his version of the Gilgamesh Epic, he called his 'Noah' Utu-napishtim, who takes a pair of each animal on board. It rains for six days and seven nights, and the flood lasts seven days before his 'ark' is stranded on Mount Nimush. Utu-napishtim sends out in turn a dove, a swallow and finally a raven, which ultimately finds land and poops on the boat. A wonderful story.

There are at least two versions of this story in the Bible. In one version, '*And of every living thing of all flesh, you shall bring two of every sort into the ark, to keep them alive with you; they shall be male and female.* ' (Genesis 6.19), in another it says, '*Take with you seven pairs of all clean animals, the male and his mate; and a pair of the animals that are not clean, the male and his mate*' (Genesis 7.2). '*The flood continued forty days upon the earth*' says one version (Genesis 7.17), '*and the waters prevailed on the earth 150 days*' in another version, before the ark is stranded on Mount Ararat (Genesis 7.24).

The creation story and the Deluge are already present in the ancient myths of Mesopotamia and was taken over into the Bible. It might become clear now, why there is talk of a flood and an ark in a rather remote and water-scarce mountain region around Jerusalem.

The story of the Flood in the Koran has only been passed down in a short version, according to which Noah is mocked by the unbelievers while building his ark. '*Embark therein, of each kind two, male and female, and your family – except those against whom the word has already gone forth – and the Believers*', it says there (Sura

11, 40). At least in the Koran Noah and his family were not the only survivors. However, there is no indication of the duration of the Flood, but the ark eventually lands on Mount al-Gudi, in the north-east of present-day Turkey. Anyone who takes the effort to read the Bible and the Koran together will quickly realize that there are many more similarities than differences. Good stories never die out.

Another task of the authors was to bring together different founding myths into one story. This includes, for example, the story of the origin of Abraham and the twelve tribes of Israel, who originally came from Mesopotamia, immediately followed by the story of the Exodus from Egypt under Moses. Two myths in one and the same story, and nobody had a problem with it. Even that Moses was abandoned in a basket on the Nile is a myth comparable to that of Romulus and Remus or Hansel and Gretel. It is the stories about dealing with unwanted children who are abandoned in nature in the hope that someone will take care of them.

Some people have had difficulties with Moses' wife, anyway. Moses' wife was black and came from Kush, roughly the Sudan of today (Numbers 12.1). And whoever complained about it was punished with leprosy, at least that's what the Bible says. The fruit of his loins was therefore at least very colourful, which is probably difficult to digest for many still today. Moses' wife, however, was also called Zipporah (Exodus 2.21), and was the daughter of a priest from

Midian, where Moses had fled after just having slained an Egyptian and buried him in the sand.

The question remains whether Moses had one wife or two, was she a Kushite or a priest's daughter or both, or was there more than one Moses? It is so easy to get confused.

Many stories in the Bible exist in more than one version, as we have seen, and the rib story is the most striking. It says '*So God created man in his own image, in the image of God he created him; male and female he created them*' (Genesis 1.27). And only a little later it says '*and the rib which the Lord God had taken from the man he made into a woman and brought her to the man*' (Genesis 2.22). It is not only theologians who heavily argue about which version to take. In a strongly patriarchal society, of course, the story with the rib is considered correct.

This is where the story of Lilith comes in, who was often referred to as the first wife of Adam, especially in the Middle Ages. This killed two birds with one stone, as Lilith was created at the same time as Adam, but could not father any offspring. Adam's second wife, Eve, was therefore cut from his rib and could finally procreate. How to express the degree of relationship to his own rib is at least, say, complicated.

However, Lilith is mentioned in Isaiah as a desert dweller: '*...and there Lilith will lurk and find her resting place*' (Isaiah 34.14). However, that Lilith was also a goddess from Sumerian mythology, called Lilu, who appears more frequently especially in Jewish mythology.

Another example is the story of the bride sold, of which exist three versions and contains a hair-raising family story. In the first version (Genesis 12.10-20), Abram and Sarai move to Egypt as economic migrant. Because Abram is afraid for his life, he pretends to be Sarai's brother. Sarai becomes the Pharaoh's wife and lives for some time in this extraordinary triangular relationship. Of course, the Pharaoh finds out the truth and confronts the couple. But instead of thinking of revenge, he makes Abram and Serai wealthy people and sends them home. Perhaps he was glad to get rid of them, who knows.

In the second version (Genesis 20), both are now called Abraham and Sarah, and both move to the south country, this time to Abimelech. The story repeats itself almost word by word. Abraham pretends to be Sarah's brother, Abimelech marries Sarah, finds out the truth and confronts them both. This time, however, Abraham admits that Sarah is in fact his half-sister on his father's side, before both receive rich gifts and leave. This remarks lead us to a family history that could not be more wired.

Abram's father had three sons, Abram, Nahor and Haran, and a daughter, Sarah, whom he had fathered with another woman. Haran, we learn, had a son named Lot and two daughters, Iscah and Milcah. Abram marries Sarah, his half-sister, who became interim wife to Abimelech. Nahor, his brother, marries Milcah, his niece (Genesis 11.27-31). Lot, Abrams nephew, later on moves with his family to Sodom, where he is warned by two angels that Sodom is to be destroyed.

The inhabitants of the city come to his house and demand the surrender of the two angels so that they can pimp their buttocks. Of course, Lot cannot allow this and offers his two virgin daughters as a substitute. *'Where are the men who came to you tonight? Bring them out to us, that we may know them '* (...) *'I beg you, my brothers, do not act so wickedly. Behold, I have two daughters who have not known any man. Let me bring them out to you, and do to them as you please. Only do nothing to these men, for they have come under the shelter of my roof'* (Genesis 19.4-8).

What his virgin daughters may have thought of this is unknown, however, some time later on the run, shortly after Lot's wife has turned into a pillar of salt - who could blame her for that - his two daughters get her father Lot drunk on two consecutive days and made him inseminate them (Genesis 19.32-38). The offsprings of these incestuous encounter later formed the tribes of the Moabites and Ammonites, yet another creation myth.

We leave this story without comment and come to the third version of the sold bride (Genesis 26.6-11). There, Abraham and Sarah finally have a son named Isaac. After Abram has fathered Isaac's half-brother, for he had in the meantime fathered a son Ishmael with Hagar, the Egyptian maidservant of Sarai, after he has thus proverbially sent his first son into the desert, Sarah dies.

While Abraham now takes care of the funeral, the son takes care of Rebekah in mother's tent (Genesis 24.67). The next famine comes, and because it seems to have worked out so well before, this time Isaac and his new wife Rebekah move in with Abimelech, with whom his parents had already lodged.

The story proceeds like both previous versions. Isaac fears for his life, pretends to be Rebekah's brother, Abimelech happens to pass by, looks through the window and thus finds out the secret of the two (Genesis 26.8). It is not known what Abimelech had seen, but probably enough to assume that it was not brother and sister. We learn from this to close the shutters if you live on the ground floor and want to have a good time.

If the different use of the names Abram and Abraham, or Sarah and Sarai, causes confusion, it is surely due to the mixing of different versions of the same story into one and the same body of text. The Bible is full of such marvellous stories, which are somehow inappropriate for children, as the protagonists violate all the laws that are found elsewhere in the Bible. So let's take a closer look at them.

Biblesex

There are three excessive references to forbidden sexual acts or relationships. In the Book of Leviticus, the Lord first forbids sexual intercourse between blood relatives. Then, however, the authors felt it necessary to go into more detail (Leviticus 18.7-23): '*You must not uncover your father's nakedness, which is your mother's nakedness. She is your mother; you must not have sexual contact with her'*, begins the list, followed by the step-mother, sister, half-sister, granddaughter, aunt, daughter-in-law or sister-in-law, which already covers the immediate family circle, and one might wonders what comes next. Well, obviously some 'threesomes' were also forbidden, namely sexual intercourse with a woman together with her daughter or granddaughter, but nothing is said about other encounters.

Also forbidden was sex with the wife's sister as long as the own wife is still alive, sex during menstru-ation, with one's neighbour, homosexual relations, and, above all, no sex with animals, because that is something only 'the others' do.

That such a clear and precise definition was neces-sary as to which sexual intercourse was permitted and which was forbidden makes today's readers wonder a little.

One should think that everything had been suffi-ciently clarified, but immediately after follows anoth-er enumeration of sexual contacts that are punishable, interestingly less detailed and in a different order (Leviticus 20.10). *'If a man commits adultery with the wife of his neighbor, both the adulterer and the adulteress shall surely be put to death'*, the list begins this time.

Now follow mother, mother-in-law, daughter--in-law, homosexual relations, sex with wife and mother at the same time, and sex with animals. Only after the animals now follow a whole series of other sexual acts made punishable, like with sisters and half-sisters, sex during menstruation, with the aunt and the sister-in-law.

That should finally be enough, the reader might think, but all good things come in threes, the authors may have thought (Deut 27. 20-23). This time, however, the list begins with '*Cursed be anyone who lies with his father's wife*', followed immediately by the obligatory animals, before sister, half-sister and mother-in-law are mentioned.

It seems a bid strange, to say it mildly, that there are repeated references to the forbidden sexual intercourse with animals. Probably this is due to the low population density or the lonely life of the rural population, but perhaps it is also due to the fact that young men had no other possibility for sexual encounters before the age of thirty, who knows.

Anyway, all three passages differ in the number of offences and the order in which they are listed. It is three different sources in one book. Most people did not notice this anyway, as only a few men could read and write.

Perhaps, the only harmless biblical quotation from the first books of Moses is in Deuteronomy 23.13: '*And you shall have a shovel with your tools, and when you sit down outside, you shall dig a hole with it and turn back and cover up your excrement*', what means as much as if you go out for a poo, don't forget the spade.

The sheep 'Daisy'

The story of the angels in Sodom and their pending 'feminisation' leads on a very special trail, and back to the law texts found on clay tablets from Mesopotamia. Of course, we do not know what the relationship between the two angels was. Nevertheless, the question arises why in the Bible story the inhabitants of the city of Sodom gather in front of Lot's house and demand the mass rape of the two men. Now, in legal texts of Mesopotamia, a provision has been found that says:

> *'If a man has intercourse with his comrade and they prove the charges against him and find him guilty, they should sodomize him and castrate him'.*

You might judge yourself what you think of this and how to bring this in line with the Bible story. In addition to these laws, however, there are also omens, and there it says:

> *'If a man has anal sex with his social equal, that man will be foremost among his brothers and colleagues'.*

It is yet unclear whether this was not meant rather as a joke, and the man should walk in front of all others, since no one liked to turn his backside towards him.

Other law texts talk of similar regulations as those, that could be found in the Bible. Sex with the mother, the daughter or between father and son was forbidden, as well as sex with the mother-in-law, at least as long as the father was still alive. The same was true for the sister-in-law, at least as long the brother was still alive. Whenever he died, the brother or, in case he also dies, the father shall take the widow. All of the sudden, the story of Tamer and Juda comes to our mind and mingles with Lot's history in Sodom.

If you already wondered about forbidden and permitted threesomes in the Bible text, well, you also find them in the Hittite laws. There it says:

> *'If brothers sleep with a free woman, it is not an offence. If father and son sleep with the same female slave or prostitute, it is not and offence'.*

> *'If a free man sleeps with a slave woman who have the same mother and with their mother, it is not an offence'.*

You may try to figure out yourself what that means. The rape of women was also the subject of legislation, even if it seems strange to us today. If a man seizes a woman in the mountains (and rapes her), it is the man's offence, but if he seizes her in her house, it is the woman's offence; the woman shall die. Probably because in the city she could have called for help. It is always amazing what problems the people of that time had to deal with, but it gets even worse.

What already seems strange in the Bible when it comes to the topic of sex with animals, takes on an even cruder twist on the ancient clay tablets, for on them we find the following stipulations:

If a man has sexual relations with a cow, it is an unpermitted sexual pairing; he will be put to death.

If a man has sexual relations with a sheep, it is an unpermitted sexual pairing; he will be put to death.

If anyone has sexual relations with a pig or a dog, he shall die.

One does not even want to know exactly what sexual hardships parts of the population of that time faced. The life for cow, sheep and pig herders seems to have been quite lonely. However, some animals obviously faced the same sexual needs towards humans, because it goes even further:

If an ox leaps on a man (in sexual excitement), the ox shall die, the man shall not die. They shall substitute one sheep for the man and put it to death.

If a pig leaps on a man (in sexual excitement), it is not an offence.

Unintentionally, images now flit through one's mind that one did not want to be there at all, and the job as a Shepard seems to have involved some serious dangers. One would like to hope that this clarifies the facts to some extent, but apparently there were also 'relationships' that were quite acceptable:

> *If a man has sexual relations with either a horse or a mule, it is not an offence, but he shall not approach the king, nor shall he become a priest.*

For some, a vivid imagination now switches on unintentionally, and a series of unwanted sequences with very dubious protagonists appear before the reader's inner eye. Inevitably, Woody Allen's film 'What you always wanted to know about sex' comes to mind, in which the lightly dressed sheep Daisy in black lingerie is so longingly adored by her human lover.

Before fantasies runs wild, it is time to take a deep breath and look at what we already have. It's safe to say that the Bible is no ordinary book. It is a work composed of an astonishingly large amount of different stories that have been edited, adapted and changed again and again over the centuries.

The creation story, the deluge and many other stories and law texts are rooted in the ancient myths and texts of Mesopotamia. They are intermingled with many other foundational myths and stories of different origins, which often stand side by side in parallel.

The view that the Bible was a 'holy book' did not emerge until centuries later. The Bible does not itself claim to have been written by a deity. It is not a catechism, nor does it give advice on how to deal with all the moral problems that are repeatedly raised. Its stories often deal with all too human problems, incest, betrayal, rape, murder, and many other not exactly juvenile incidents.

In the 'Old Testament' there is no hell, no resurrection, no immortal soul, and no afterlife. All these ideas had their origins in Persia and Greece, and were only later adopted in Christianity and the 'New Testament'.

However, parts of the 'Old Testament' also describe the historical development of the region. They are consistent with the finds that Botta and Layard discovered during their excavations. So it's worth taking a look at that, too.

I suggest a small café somewhere in the Levant, from where we have a good overview of what was actually going on when essential parts of the 'Old Testament' were written together. Let's go to the Café Levante ...

Stories from the Levant

Café Levant

Welcome to the Café Levante, take a seat and order a delicious cold drink before we take a closer look at the scenery. We are in the last half of the eighth century B.C., and it's an exciting period loaded with Egyptians, Assyrians and Babylonians. Within the next two hundred years, none of these empires mentioned in the Bible will have survived, and all of it without any 'Sea Peoples'.

'Israel' currently consists of a northern kingdom of Israel and a southern kingdom of Judah. Egypt initially dominated the region, but due to internal power struggles they will not to re-enter history until the Black Pharaohs of Kush. The Assyrian Empire, with its new capital at Kalchu, or Nimrud, where Layard discovered the stone pyramid, slowly but steadily re-emerged as a superpower in the region. Massive settlement programmes were implemented, and alone king Tiglatpileser III resettled sixty-five thousand people from the Zagros region. He extended his domain far to the west, and when he finally subjugated Babylon, the Assyrians were once again the number one in the region.

So let us first take a look towards the east, from where now, around 733 BC, a huge cloud of dust is rolling in. The small city-states in the Levant had tried to forge an alliance against the increasingly strong Assyrian. However, not everyone complied. King Ahaz, Assyria's ally from the southern kingdom of Judah, called on Tiglatpileser for help, who gratefully accepted this invitation. The military power now rushing past us brings almost the entire Levant under its control, deports parts of the population, and makes the countries of the Levant pay tribute. A long period of peace on the Mediterranean has ended. '*In the days of Pekah king of Israel, Tiglathpileser king of Assyria came and captured Ijon, Abel-beth-maacah, Janoah, Kedesh, Hazor, Gilead, and Galilee, all the land of Naphtali, and he carried the people captive to Assyria*', says the Bible (2 Kings 15.29). Assyrian sources prove that Hoshea, not Pekah, was king. There is some disagreement about this issue.

Instead of keeping calm, Hoschea from the northern kingdom of Israel revolted against his new master. The kings messenger is just trotting south past us to ask the Pharaoh for support against the Assyrians. It was in vain, however, Egypt was not yet ready. When Hoshea then stopped his tribute payments, another dusty cloud appeared on the horizon in the morning of 722 BC, this time even more powerful than the first one. It's time for a new cold drink, the day is promising.

This time the Assyrian king's name was Sargon II. He was the ruler who had moved his capital to Dûr-Sharrûkin, the place north of Mosul that Botta had mistakenly believed to be ancient Nineveh. Sargon had brought new settlers with him, for he was thinking of a somewhat larger resettlement operation.

Hoshea, of course, had no chance. According to Assyrian sources, Sargon took nearly thirty thousand prisoners into his kingdom, and integrated two hundred chariots into his army. Stonemasons expanded Samaria and made it an Assyrian province, the new citizens who had previously been brought in large numbers were settled in the city, and a general was appointed as governor. We know all this from the Kalah prism that Botta had excavated in Dûr-Sharrûkin.

The story of the lost 'Ten Tribes of Israel' from the Bible seems to have started here. It begins with Esau, Jacob and a lentil soup, in which Jacob later marries his two cousins, goes to bed with their slaves as well, and from his twelve children by four wives spring the 'Twelve Tribes of Israel' (Genesis 25.29). Where the ten tribes are resettled, however, is not clear. The Bible only says: '*In the ninth year of Hoshea, the king of Assyria captured Samaria, and he carried the Israelites away to Assyria and placed them in Halah, and on the Habor, the river of Gozan, and in the cities of the Medes*' (2 Kings 17:6).

After the dust has settled and everything is nicely rebuilt, it's time for a little overview. The northern kingdom of Israel no longer exists, and in the southern kingdom of Judah there was a veritable population explosion, probably also because many inhabitants of the north had fled here.

It was probably the time when the many different versions of some Bible stories came together, brought along by the groups that had fled, each with their own version of one and the same story. It could well be the time that the different founding myths came together, that from now on three versions of the sold bride in Jerusalem were told, and that each group brought its own legislation with it.

In any case, oil and wine production took off, and the first camel caravans were now heading towards Arabia. Perhaps one of them was carrying young Joseph to sell him to Egypt. The coastal cities flourished, Jerusalem became a real city, and everything could have been nice and easy.

Why king Hezekiah suddenly decided to rebel against Assyria remains a mystery. It was probably this Hezekiah who first intended to impose the belief in one God only and set the writers of the Bible the task of eradicating all other gods from the ancient epics.

In Egypt, meanwhile, the Kushite pharaohs had prevailed. Pharaoh Shabaka secretly supported the cities of the Levant in their rebellion against the Assyrians. Sargon's successor Sanherib, meanwhile, had quite different problems to solve with Babylon, with whom there were repeated tensions. The dust clouds that are soon approaching are enormous. Time to order a new drink and see what happens next in this boiling pot.

First, around 701 BC, smoke rises before our eyes, evidence of a rebellion. Again, a horseman trots out of the mountains southwards to the Pharaoh to ask for help, and this time Egypt is ready. On the eastern horizon, a really massive dust cloud rises this time, indicating that Sanherib is pretty pissed and on the move. To the south we see a dust cloud in which a young Kushite prince named Taharqa is leading his troops north. Finally, something is happening in the Middle East.

Over the next few hours, there is a tremendous clatter before our eyes. As the fog of battle gradually lifts, we can see Prince Taharqa fleeing home at lightning speed and barricading himself there, as the Assyrian war machine slowly mills its way through the city walls of Lachish. An image that Sanherib had made for his new capital, Nineveh, and which was excavated by Layard two and a half thousand years later.

Now two versions come into play. The biblical one speaks of the subjugation of Hezekiah, king of Jerusalem, and the payment of three hundred talents of silver and thirty talents of gold as tribute (2 Kings 18.14). However, Sanherib cannot take Jerusalem because the LORD destroys the whole Assyrian army (2 Kings 19.35). The Assyrian version, however, speaks of a massive campaign against the southern kingdom of Judah. '*I besieged and captured forty-six of his fortified cities, along with many smaller towns, taken in battle with my battering rams. I took as plunder 200,150 people, both small and great, male and female, along with a great number of animals including horses, mules, donkeys, camels, oxen, and sheep*' is stated on a Prism. Sanherib accordingly imprisons Hezekiah '*like a bird in a cage*' in Jerusalem and eventually leaves him to continue in office as a vassal of Assyria. In addition, he took Hezekiah's daughters, his harem, jewels, ivory, thirty talents of gold and eight hundred talents of silver as tribute to his capital Nineveh. You are free to choose which story they like the most.

However, the Assyrian king probably did not show interest in further conquests. His problem remained Babylon. After a long siege, Babylon was finally conquered, the city was razed to the ground and the Tigris channelled through the middle of it.

Sanherib built Nineveh into a new residence. Canal systems, tunnels and aqueducts of one hundred and fifty kilometres length were built to bring water in from distant areas. The Jerwan Aqueduct spanned a valley two hundred and eighty metres wide. Entire floodplains were created to protect against floods and as huge water reservoirs where animals from all over the empire were settled for hunting. It was the heyday of the Assyrians.

Probably Sanheribs sons did not quite agree with his choice of successor, so they took the problem into their own hands and assassinated him. After six months of civil war, his youngest son Asarhaddon finally prevailed, a young man who consistently carried on the family tradition. At first, he beheaded those family members whom he believed could be dangerous to him. Once he had decimated them sufficiently, he began his annual campaigns and, incidentally, had Babylon rebuilt.

In Egypt, Prince Taharqa had meanwhile become Pharaoh, and created an elite force that could be proud of itself. Near his residence in Memphis, he had his soldiers take part in a nightly ultramarathon across the desert to the Great Lake Birket Qarun and back.

There '*the king himself, on horseback, watched his soldiers run as he exercised with them in the desert behind Memphis at the ninth hour of the night. They reached the Great Lake at the hour of sunrise and returned to the residence at the third hour of day*'. That's almost one hundred kilometres in eight hours, in full gear and across the desert sands. An achievement that also had to be recorded on a stele.

About 2700 years later, the Egyptian Mahmud Ali Dehais won the newly held desert race with a time of 8:35:20 hours to commemorate the achievements of that time. However, no stele was erected in his honour. He was only worth a small article in a local newspaper. Some things just relativise over time.

A Pharao with such an excellent army will certainly make use of it. So, the already familiar picture now emerges. In 671 BC we become aware of a dust cloud with Taharqa's desert warriors in the south, and another one with Asarhaddon's war machines in the east. Actually, a heroic battle should now follow, but this time everything happens surprisingly fast.

The Assyrian king did not flinch for long and was so quickly in front of Egypt's capital that Taharqa fled helter-skelter to the south, leaving everything behind, including his family. On his way back to Niniveh Asarhaddon had the entire Egyptian court with him as prisoners. '*His queen, his harem, Prince Ushankhuru his inheritance and the rest of his sons and daughters, his property and goods, his horses, his cattle, his sheep in innumerable quantities I led to Assyria. The roots of Kush I plucked out of Egypt*', he noted on a victory stele which can be seen today in the Pergamon Museum in Berlin.

The Kushite rule over Egypt had just come to an end. The next Assyrian king, Ashurbanipal, ensured peace in his new province. His most exciting legacy is probably his library, where more than two thousand years later Layard and his colleague Rassam unearthed those clay tablets that George Smith deciphered in the British Museum as the Gilgamesh Epic. Around sixty years had passed since the first appearance of Tiglatpileser, Egypt seemed to be defeated and the Assyrians had won. But the story is not that simple after all as we will see.

For now, relax, and listen to the fairy tale of Cinderella during our well-deserved lunch break. Not the version that you all know, but the one that the Greeks and Egyptians told, the original Cinderella, so to speak. You'd better order something stronger, it's getting a bit delicate.

Cinderella for adults

Cinderella is widely known as the innocent young lady who loses her shoe and thus becomes the prince's consort. A beautiful and widespread story that is still read to children today. The ancient Greek version, however, is about Rhodopis, the most famous hetaera in the world at that time, who had opened a brothel in Egypt's most colourful city, Naukratis. The storyteller Herodotus, who is now being mentioned more and more frequently, virtually raved about the beauty and permissiveness of the women of this town. Sex tourism to southern countries probably already existed in antiquity.

Rhodopis, who according to her name was rosy in appearance, originally came to Naukratis as the sex slave of the Samian Xanthos. She met Charaxos, the brother of the famous Greek poet Sappho, who was later said to found the lesbian love on the island of Lesbos. Charaxos fell madly in love with the young woman, and after a long bargain with the Samian, he bought Rhodopis free for a considerable huge sum.

The laughter at him was understandably great, for Rhodopis did not go back to Thrace, where she was born, but remained in the city as an independent entrepreneur earning a fortune in the horizontal business. Out of sheer gratitude, she later donated part of her money to the temple of Delphi in the form of huge roasting spits on which oxen could be roasted. Apparently, Delphi also knew how to celebrate lavish parties.

But lets go back to the story. According to Strabon, a later writer, a shoe was stolen from Rhodopis by an eagle while she was taking a refreshing bath in a nearby river. The eagle flew away with the stolen shoe and dropped it on the head of the pharaoh. He immediately sent out a search for the wearer of the shoe, fell madly in love with her and finally married her.

So we can consider the noble prostitute Rhodopis, the most famous hetaera of the ancient world, as the ancestor of that Cinderella we still encounter in children's stories today. Whether Walt Disney will ever bring this ancient version to the market as an animated film seems rather doubtful.

Prostitution was part of everyday life in antiquity, and Corinth was known for its many brothels. Anyone who 'Corinthised' went to a prostitute, such as the young Neaira, who was bought and trained as a slave by a brothel owner at a young age. At the height of her professional career, around her early twenties, she was sold to two regular customers as a sex slave, a transaction that must have been quite common at the time. She was later charged with professional adultery, according to trial records that survived the centuries.

Anyone caught in the act of adultry, however, faced a hefty penalty. It could happen to the adulterer that the betrayed husband took revenge with a relish, and carefully 'feminised' the offender with a radish. And while the root vegetable slowly penetrated his backside, his pubic hair was torn out one by one, before finally the remaining rectal areas were singed off with an open flame. All this can be read in Aristophanes' comedy 'The Clouds'. Some scholars even suspect that instead of the radish, one or the other poisonous scorpion fish was introduced into the offender's rectum. However, there is no evidence for this. Fortunately.

The Greek poet Xenarchos draws attention to what strict draconian rules by saying: '*How, Aphrodite, do they ever manage to fuck married women, thinking of the laws of Dracon?*' I am only the bearer of the words, nothing more.

In any case, the topic of sex and prostitution was omnipresent in antiquity. The reason lay in the general living situation, which has already been described. Only male descendants could inherit from their fathers, and thus did not have the opportunity to start a family until they were about thirty years old. Until then, many of them could only gain sexual experience with prostitutes. Or animals, who knows. For many women, it was one of the few opportunities to earn money to support themselves.

Moral reservations, as they exist today, were therefore few. The romantic idea of marriage and the view that every man and woman should be allowed to marry and start a family originated only in the nineteenth century.

Young women, for example, who until then worked as servants in the household of a wealthy fellow citizen, were usually denied any contact with men, and marriage could only take place with the consent of the head of the household.

However, there is the suspicion that some scholars of antiquity are so fond of their subject only because so many ancient pornographic depictions and erotic narratives that have been found.

Probably the oldest known sex graffiti comes from Egypt in the fifteenth, pre-Christian century. It is located very close to the temple of Hatshepsut near Thebes. It shows the pharaoh in what can be described as a 'conversation' in the broadest sense of the word with her chief temple builder. Unfortunately, the worker who probably expressed his displeasure with his clients here, remains unnamed.

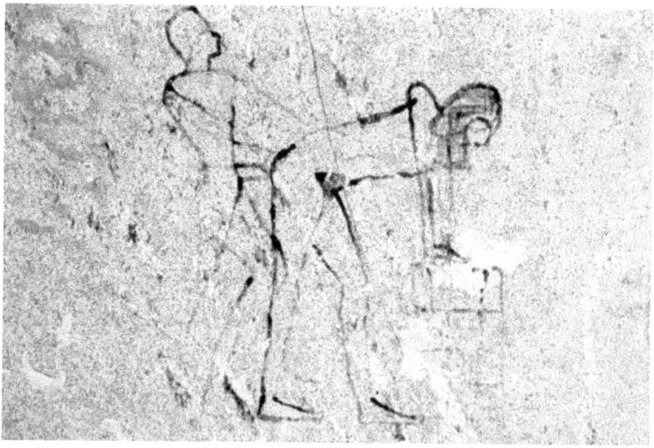

At the beginning of the nineteenth century, a papyrus was found near Deir el Medine in Egypt that shocked the experts of the time. After Jean-François Champollion had seen the papyrus in Turin in 1824, he wrote a letter to his brother in which he expressed his horror at '*the depiction of monstrous obscenity*', which left him with '*a very strange impression of Egyptian wisdom and spirituality*'.

What Champollion had just seen was probably the oldest porno in worlds history – at least on paper. The erotic depictions in the so-called 'Turin Papyrus', are peppered with lascivious comments, and probably also demonstrate the first intercourse in a car, as one can see.

Of course, this papyrus remained under lock and key in the museum's cellars. Only selected people, and of course only men, had access to it at all.

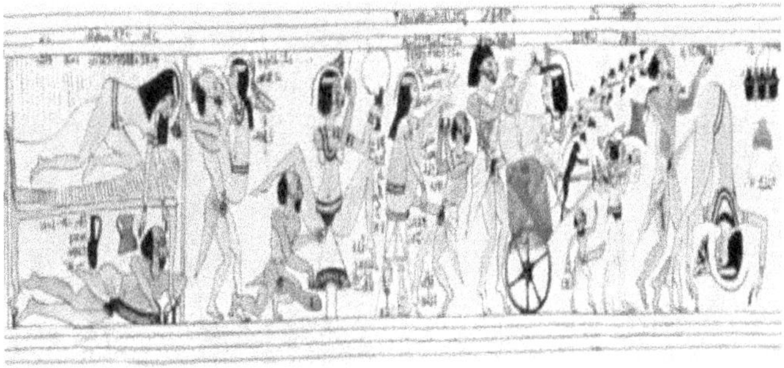

Finally, in Mesopotamia, it was above all the numerous clay tablets that puzzled the research community. Unfortunately, it is not known what both Botta and Layard may have been thinking when they came across the many small clay plaques during the excavations, on which a woman is drinking beer with a straw from a carafe during the act, seemingly unimpressed. But some also argue she is about to throw up.

All this contradicts our modern sexual ideas, of course, which are more 'Victorian', and in which a Lady Hillingdon reports on her married life: '*When I hear his steps outside my door, I lie down on my bed, open my legs and think of England*'. Whether the saying really originated with her is uncertain. What was certain, however, was the completely uptight attitude to sexuality that prevailed at the time.

So let's leave sex alone, end our little lunch break and return to our history. With our cultural upbringing, we can probably cope better with accounts of people chopping off each other's limbs and slaughtering each other a thousand times over.

It's hard to imagine what it would look like if some ten thousand warriors met on a huge battlefield and suddenly went into a huge orgy. 'Make Love not War' would take on a whole new dimension. Well, let there be blood and guts spraying, and keep on with our story.

Va pensiro - Babylon

Actually, the story seems to be almost finished. In the mountainous highlands of the Levant, people were busy composing their original Bible, and Babylon, Egypt and the entire Levant was under Assyrian rule. The New Assyrian Empire was at the height of its power. It was the first world empire in history, only that world empires have a silly habit of going down, strangely enough always when it is at its best, and at spiralling speed.

The end of Ashurbanipal's reign already indicates some difficulties as there are hardly any reliable sources. To the north, the Lydian Empire came under pressure, and their king Gyges is said to have asked for Assyrian support.

The only evidence is that Babylonian troops from the south and Median troops from the east put an end to the Assyrian empire. In 614 BC Assur fell, and in July 612 BC Nineveh was taken. '*A city, though small and built on a remote rock, is better than foolish Nineveh*', Phocylides from Greek Miletus later wrote. The fall of Nineveh shook the world of that time.

Shortly afterwards, the armies of Babylon and the Medes stood before the last remaining Assyrian stronghold of Harran. The Egyptian vassal was still supposed to help the Assyrians in battle, but it was in vain. He was no longer able to prevent the final downfall of the Assyrians. One hundred and thirty years had passed since Tiglatpileser III, and Babylon and Egypt were suddenly on top again.

The new Babylonian king, Nabopolassar, was probably a renegade Assyrian general, which is probably why the fall of Nineveh had happened so fast. If the name Nabopolassar doesn't ring a bell, his successor Nebuchadnezzar certainly does. In 597 BC, he marched past our café in the direction of Jerusalem, conquered the city and deported the Judean king Jehoiakin, who actually appeared in the ration lists of the palace administration in Babylon. However, it is unclear whether the Babylonian captured Jerusalem again ten years later and deported the population.

According to the Bible, however, this is the time when the Southern Kingdom of Judah fell and became part of the New Babylonian Empire. So if the deportation of the Jews did not take place at all, it is one of those founding myths that was supposed to give a rather motley community a common identity.

However the history was like, what remains is the 'va pensiero' of the prisoners' chorus from Guiseppe Verdi's opera Nabucco. A story about the desire for freedom of the Jews in exile and written in 1841 AD, when people in Italy were rebelling against the old order and calling for their own nation state in patriotic exuberance. Nabucco is an Italian opera about the situation of 'Italy', that should not be forgotten.

The end of the New Babylonian Empire is quickly told. It went the way of everything earthly and ended as quickly as it had appeared. The last Babylonian king, Nabonid, must have lost interest after some time, preferring instead to stay in the oasis city of Teima on the Arabian Peninsula.

He did not realise that the Persian king Cyrus was soon to put an end to his rule. Less than eighty years after the Assyrians, the second great empire had now disappeared from the map, and still there were no 'Sea Peoples' in sight. Its remains were rediscovered more than two thousand years later. Egypt was the last candidate of the biblical empires. Verdi is already sitting in front of his piano, composing his next opera from the end of its history.

Aida's end

It has already been a long day here in the café, and it won't take long any more. Greeks will appear on the scene even more now, and where there are old Greeks, things are often a bit more funny and hearty. Order your last drink, the end will come quickly.

Already under Assyrian rule, Psammtek I was appointed Pharaoh and had built up a huge army of mercenaries. The Lydian king Gyges is said to have become filthy rich in this business, for if 'Greece' had another lucrative export product besides oil and wine, it was well-trained mercenaries, who were now also to be found in the upper ranks of the Egyptian military.

Psammtek's successor Necho II was already dealing with the Babylonians. We see the familiar dust clouds passing by again and again, from east to south and back again, but it becomes increasingly boring.

The most interesting event probably was a fleet the Pharaoh let built and sail around Africa, as Herodotus reports. When the expedition passed Gibraltar after three years to enter into the Mediterranean, the pharaoh had already died and his successor Psammtek II faced a completely different problem.

By the way, about one hundred years later, a new sailing expedition under the Persian Sataspes is said to have started, also with the aim of sailing around Africa, writes the same Herodotus. However, the expedition was aborted and Sataspes was nailed to the cross after his return. Actually, he was not crucified because of his failure, but because he was said to have raped a virgin from higher circles. His mother had then lobbied the Persian king Xerxes and was able to exchange his immediate death for an extended cruise. She was the king's aunt, and Sataspes therefore Xerxes' cousin. Apparently, however, the young man had no desire for swaying seas, broke off the journey, returned prematurely and thus ended his life in unpleasantly lofty heights on a cross. Sometimes, it seems, you are really punished with your relatives. But back to the story.

Psammtek's problem were the Kushites in the south. So now we see a dusty cloud heading there. The Egyptian, Greek and Jewish mercenaries quickly carve their names into the statues of Ramses II, before causing a bloodbath and wading in a river of excrements and intestines, as it says on a stele. Now there was peace in the south, and the pharaoh had all references to the time of the black pharaohs destroyed.

For Guiseppe Verdi it was an inspiration. He pulled out his pencil and composed his opera 'Aida', in which the Ethiopian king's daughter Aida is taken hostage to Egypt.

Psammtek's successor Apries was later overthrown by the former general Amasis, who declared himself Pharaoh. Apries immediately sent a messenger named Patarbemis to the apostate general with a request to appear before him immediately. '*But when Patarbemis arrived and summoned Amasis before the king'*, writes Herodotus, '*Amasis - he was sitting on horseback at the time - rose up in the saddle and sent a wind: let him bring this to Apries*'. I'm just warning you in advance, because Herodotus, the so-called 'Father of History', sometimes exaggerates a bid, but you will get him to know later. He goes on to report that the royal flatulence so upset the former Pharaoh Apries that he had cut off the messenger's ears and nose. To keep a long story short, Amasis became Pharaoh and took Ladike, a young Greek woman from Cyrene as his wife, Herodotus reports.

He seemed to have suffered from acute potency problems as he was unable to copulate with his young wife, while he was able to do so with other women, we learn from Herodotus. As this continued for a some time, Amasis said to Ladice: '*Woman, thou hast certainly bewitched me - now therefore be sure thou shalt perish more miserably than ever woman perished yet'*.

Ladice was spared, and unfortunately we don't know what kind of potency she had mixed into her old husband's wine. In any case, the pharaoh got his money's worth the next night and immediately dedicated a statue of Aphrodite, the goddess of love, to the city. Ladice became so famous that night that even the Persian king Cambyses left her unscathed when he conquered Egypt a short time later.

She was probably as clueless as Rhodopis in her brothel, unaware of what was brewing in the East. With the Persians a tsunami was now rushing over Babylon, Egypt and all the other empires, who fell into the hands of the Persians, sometimes without spilling a single drop of blood.

Egypt's last pharaoh, Psammtek III, managed a record-breaking six months before becoming history. A sad record for the last Egyptian pharaoh. He was defeated by the forces of Cambysus at Pelusion in 525 BC. Ladice was allowed to return home unharmed, while the pharaoh was forced to commit suicide at the behest of the Persian king by drinking himself to death in public on bulls' blood. So tells us Herodotus.

It's time to order one last cold drink and take a leisurely look around. Within the last two hundred years, three great empires rose and fell again. Egypt, Assyria and Babylon ceased to exist, and all without the famous 'Sea Peoples'. Some of the stories from the Bible seem to agree with the archaeological findings.

But this does not mean that all stories of the Bible are based on historical facts. Rather, it is a collection of individual stories that have been compiled over centuries and edited again and again. It contains ancient creation and foundation myths, poems, chronicles, laws, and a multitude of morally rather questionable stories.

The Greeks were now appearing more and more frequently in the story, and it is worth asking whether the Iliad, the oldest work of Greek mythology, does not also contain some parts from the ancient epics of Mesopotamia. When we go there in a moment, we will meet with Herodotus again, as well as some philosophers who are still believed to have been the founding fathers of rational science. We will question some things again and look at how long we have been telling ourselves these stories. We will also eventually encounter some of the ideas we still believe today.

It's time to go to Greece and see, where some of these ideas came from and what effect they still have. We don't even have to go on a long journey. However, it is late, night has fallen, the stars are shining brightly over the horizon, and you've certainly had the one or other drink too much.

So relax, lean back, lift your head towards the east and look up at the sky. The rest will happen by itself, trust me...

Greek stories

Don' trust in swans with morning glory
Woman with Stockholm syndrome
Hellenic fantasies
Farting philosophers
Pre-Socratic lifestyle
Bizarre deaths in philosophy
Herodotus in Bodenwerder
Greek Symposium
Athenian triumvirate

Don't trust in swans with morning glory

On clear nights, two stars appear in the eastern sky, Castor and Pollux, and both are part of the constellation 'Gemini'. With a little imagination, you can really see two brothers holding each others hand. However, if you see the holes of a blowpipe, you are already in the Amazon, but let's don't go that far. We better stay in our realms and take a closer look at the story of Castor and Pollux.

Castor and Pollux were a very special couple in Greek mythology. I'm on the verge of apologising for the fact that it's about to get a bit more delicate again, but I'm just the bearer of the news. Please leave my nose and ears alone. So, the story of the twins begins as follows:

Zeus, the father of gods, in his almost insatiable hunger for extramarital sexual affairs, which continually infuriated his wife Hera, this Zeus once again longed for an adventure. One day he caught sight of the beautiful Leda, the wife of Tyndareos, king of Sparta. Zeus, of course, immediately fell in love with Leda and devised a way to possess and inseminate her, because when Zeus cheated, he cheated with all the consequences.

The father of the gods could of course transform himself into anything he wanted. For the beautiful Europa, he had already dressed up as a bull and kidnapped her to Crete. With the beautiful Leda, however, he devised another ruse. He turned himself into a swan pretending to be pursued and hunted by an eagle. And so he rescued himself into the arms of the beautiful Leda, who, by pure chance, was lying there completely naked and with her thighs wide open, and took him into her sheltering arms.

You can certainly imagine what followed. Not only painters like Michelangelo, Rubens and Leonardo da Vinci were inspired by this motif, but also poets like William Butler Yeats were fascinated by this story:

A sudden blow: the great wings beating still
Above the staggering girl, her thighs caressed
By the dark webs, her nape caught in his bill,
He holds her helpless breast upon his breast.
How can those terrified vague fingers push
The feathered glory from her loosening thighs?
And how can body, laid in that white rush,
But feel the strange heart beating where it lies?

And the moral of the story, don't trust in swans with morning glory. It was probably the first and hopefully the last swan in world literature with an erect male penis. It would just be too good if the story ended now, but of course it goes on.

Beautiful Leda rushes home, horrified that much after this unexpected encounter, that she also sleeps with her husband that same night. Of course she becomes pregnant, Zeus was involved. Since he had turned into a swan, Leda laid two eggs nine months later. Yes, you read correctly, this is Greek mythology at it's best.

One egg, fertilised by Zeus, the father of gods, gave birth to the most beautiful woman in the world, Helena, and the immortal Pollux. The other egg, fertilised by her husband Tyndareos, gave birth to Castor and Clytemnestra.

Castor and Pollux later sail with Jason and the Argonauts to Colchis to steal the golden fleece. Castor gets finally killed in battle, and Pollux asks his father Zeus for the immortality of his beloved brother. The father of the gods finally shows mercy, and so, today, the two stars Castor and Pollux can be seen in the eastern sky.

Meanwhile, the beautiful Helen is abducted by Paris to Troy, thus triggering the Trojan War. Her sister Clytemnestra becomes the wife of the ruler of Mycenae, King Agamemnon, who, with his army and the support of Odysseus and Archilleus, besieges Troy for ten years, of course only after he has sacrificed his daughter Iphigenia, which brings him to an evil end on his return. Clytemnestra kills him upon arrival in revenge for the murder of their common child. Iphigenia's sister in turn asks her brother Orestes to avenge her father's murder. Orestes relents and kills his mother Clytemnestra, and so ends the Mycenaean empire. Again, without any 'Sea Peoples'.

The next time you see the stars Castor and Pollux in the night sky, it should be up to you whether you see the Greek zodiac sign of Gemini, or a blowpipe from the Brazilian rainforest. It just depends where you are and which story you believe in.

In any case, the Greek version offers the ultimate introduction to Greek mythology, and thus also to Homer's story of the Iliad, which was written around the same time as the first writings of the Bible.

Welcome to Greece. I hope you had a pleasant journey.

Woman with Stockholm syndrome

Homer's work 'Iliad' was written in the 8th century BC, roughly the same time as the first stories in the Bible were compiled. The Iliad does not describe the entire ten years of the siege of Troy, but only a tiny fraction, to be more precise about fifty days of the conflict. Essentially, it is not about the conquest of the city either, but rather vast numbers of individual stories are told, of the all too human and of divine providence. The possibilities for its interpretation are as large as the text is long, and long it is in deed.

All the trouble begins with a woman, of course. We are, after all, with the ancient Greeks. But it is not about the stolen Helen, no no, but with the beautiful Briseis. Agamemnon, the leader of the Greek army, refused to set free his almond-eyed Chryseis he keeps as a sex slave, ignoring that she is the daughter of a priest of god Apollo. '*I will not free her. She shall grow old in my house at Argos far from her own home, busying herself with her loom and visiting my bed*' he fantasises.

Just to remember, Agamemnon is married to Clytemnestra, the sister of Helen, both offsprings of Zeus. He totally forgot that a Greek hero should never mess with his wife, nor with the gods. And keeping the daughter of Apollos priest as a sex slave is a very bad idea, indeed. Of course, the god sends a plague into the camp, and finally Agamemnon is forced to hand over the priest's daughter.

As compensation he demands Archilleus' own sex slave, the beautiful Briseis. A loud argument ensues, but in the end, Archilleus has to hand over his Briseis, but now refuses to take part in the fight against Troy.

The gods interfere in the battle, and they are as divided among themselves as the camp of the Greeks. On Mount Olympus, Hera insults her husband Zeus as a 'sneaky bastard', some of the gods side with the Trojans, others with the Greeks. Trouble is pre-programmed, and the slaughter on earth will not end as long as there is no agreement in heaven.

What follows is a cabinet of cruelty. Guts spill out of cut open abdomens, muscles and tendons are severed, organs are torn apart, skulls are split with the sword and brains splatter in all directions. Spears pierce breastplates or penetrate necks, shatter teeth, split tongues, and teeth bite cold bronze as the lifeless body crashes to the ground. It is the first 'splatter movie' of antiquity. Homer's audience was excited.

Only when Patroklos, Archilleus' companion, dies in battle, the hero decides to rejoin the fight. He also gets back his beautiful sex slave Briseis, who shows strong signs of the Stockholm Syndrome, in which the victim of a kidnapping builds up a 'positive emotional relationship with her captor'.

> *'I saw him to whom my father and mother married me, cut down before our city, and my three own dear brothers perished with him on the self-same day; but you, Patroklos, even when Achilles slew my husband and sacked the city of noble Mynes, told me that I was not to weep, for you said you would make Achilles marry me, and take me back with him to Phthia, we should have a wedding feast among the Myrmidons. You were always kind to me and I shall never cease to grieve for you'.*

It does sound a little cynical that the murderer of the entire family saves his last victim for his bed. But don't think that such scenes only occur among the ancient Greeks. The Bible has similar storries to offer.

The end of the Iliad is quickly told. Archilleus defeats Hector, slaughters twelve Trojan young men on the funeral pyre of his friend Patroclus, and finally King Pergamon appears to request the desecrated body of his son, which still lies unburied in the field.

Thus ends Homer's story of the Trojan War, without any Trojan horse, and without the conquest of Troy. These stories, in fact, are told in the so-called Epic Cycle. Homer's Iliad and his Odyssey are only two parts of a much larger story, which unfortunately have only survived in fragments. This includes the Kypria, which is still of interest to us.

In the Enuma Elis, and the Atrahasis, the trouble always began with the fact that it had become too crowded and too noisy on earth. The Greek Kypria has a 'pre-song', or rather an introduction, which clearly refers to these ancient epics:

> *'There was a time when the countless nations roaming over the land threatened to crush the broad and wide breast of the earth; zeus saw this and took pity; in his wise counsel he resolved to deliver the all-nourishing earth from the weight of humanity by unleashing the great battles of the trojan war to have their heavy burden lightened by death: so the warriors were slain before troia, so zeus' will was fulfilled'.*

The decimation of the population through famine, pestilence and war are already part of many ancient stories from Mesopotamia. There are clear connections between Greek literature and the ancient stories from Mesopotamia, even if they are not as striking as in the Bible. The parallels are not by chance, for there were quite close relations between the Assyrian empire and some Greek cities. The Greek alphabet was 'imported' from the Levant at this time. The Mesopotamian sagas were also known to the scribes in Greece, and it almost seems as if an educated Greek like Homer, when he learned the new alphabet in the East, also had initial lessons in Oriental literature.

There are also other hints that connect the Iliad to the ancient epics of Mesopotamia. For example, when Hera seduces her husband she goes to Aphrodite, the goddess of love, and asks her for an aphrodisiac. Hera wants to go to the beginning of time, to the 'origin of the gods' and the 'origin of everything'. In doing so, she tells the story of Okeanos and Tethys, the father of all rivers and the goddess of the seas, the endless quarrel and the separation of the two. The parallels with 'Enuma Elish' and the quarrel between Apsu and Tiamat are all too clear.

The goddess Aphrodite, in turn, actually is a devine import from Mesopotamia, and no one else than the goddess Ishtar from the tales of the Gilgamesh epic, or Innana, the goddess of fertility and sexual desire, whom we had already encountered with Sîn-lēqi-unninni.

Homer's works were long considered lost, and were unknown in the Middle Ages. So it's worth asking when we started retelling this ancient story, and Göttingen University quickly comes into play again. In 1772 a Johann Heinrich Voß studied there, who a few years later was to translate Homer's ancient works into German and make them famous, especially in the literary circles of his time.

It was the time when 'the Greeks' were rediscovered and caused veritable storms of enthusiasm. We will see later how this came about and what role this university in Göttingen played in it.

Hellenic fantasies

Whatever one may think of Homer's Iliad, it is a wonderful story. However, not everyone saw it that way even back then.

Xenophanes was an ancient 'philosopher' who actually came from Colophon on today's Turkish west coast, but immediately took to his heels when the Persian king appeared outside his home town. In his late twenties, he tied his lyre under his arm, spent the next few years travelling from town to town, and tried to earn his living in the marketplaces by reciting the Homeric poetry.

After a few years of reciting the whole epic from top to bottom and back again, occurred what probably happens to many persons who earn their living by constantly doing the same again and again. Xenophanes began to hate Homer and his work! Profoundly! His disgust reached the point that he wrote his own works and mocking songs against the poet, and did not stop railing against him like the devil.

After a few years, his malice was no longer directed against Homer alone; his opinion of his audience was also beginning to leave much to be desired. '*The mass of things fall short of thought*' was one of his quotes. In his opinion, '*encounters with tyrants should be as few, or else as pleasant, as possible*', which eventually became his doom.

One of these tyrants finally could not stand his nagging any longer, took him into custody, and sold him as a slave to southern Italy.

Heraclitus of Ephesus, to whom the saying 'panta rhei' - everything flows is said to go back, was no follower of Homeric epics either. '*Homer deserved to be chased out of the lists of poets and beaten with rods*', he said. Heraclitus was rich, very rich indeed, and yet, or probably because of this, he was a real misanthrope and had even less to offer to his fellow human beings than his colleague Xenophanes.

Finally, he went to the mountains and fed on grass and herbs. '*If happiness consisted of physical pleasures*', he said once, '*one would have to call oxen happy if they found peas to eat*'. It all depends, therefore, on how you define pleasure.

Later, when he suffered from dropsy, he asked the doctors, if '*they were competent to create a drought after heavy rain*', or '*whether anyone could by emptying the intestines draw off the moisture*'. Of course, no one understood what the hell he was talking about, which probably earned him the nickname 'The Obscure'.

The water-addicted Heraclitus finally buried himself in stinking cow-dung, hoping to get the water out of his body. However, the dung dried up in the sun, whereupon Heraclitus was really deep in the shit now. He is said to have been unable to get out of it and was eaten by dogs.

Miraculously, we have arrived at Greek philosophy, a topic that often makes readers banging their heads on the edge of the table. '*The basic character of Milesian natural philosophy may be described as distinctly rational-physical*', one still reads today in some textbooks.

Of course, western philosophy started with these ancient Greeks, who had already thought everything imaginable, at least according to these authors. One could almost get the impression that for the first philosophers the discovery of nuclear fission was just a matter of time.

The whole story starts with Thales, Anaximander and Anaximenes, and words like the '*unlimited*', the '*apeiron*' or '*ta onta*' are soon slapped around ones ears. Funnily enough, their language sounds just as overblown as that of some mostly, and in particular, German philosophers more than two thousand years after them. But just take it just a little hint with a sledge hammer.

From the 'natural philosopher' Anaximander, for example, a single cryptic sentence has come down to us, and, depending on the translation, it reads as follows: '*... according to necessity; for they compensate one another and pay penance for their injustice according to the* *order of time*'. However, no one knows what this means, and yet to this day it is claimed that he was '*the first among all men to produce a purely physical cosmogony*' and produced '*a history of the origin of our cosmos based exclusively on observation and purely rational thought*'.

Once again, it is worth asking where these views come from, and let's take a look at the works of those 'philosophers' who lived before Socrates. Well, it's quite easy, there are none. Original writings have not survived, and the knowledge about these jokers consists of reports and fragments that were mostly produced between a hundred and a thousand years later. If one looks at what was written about them in antiquity, it doesn't get any better.

Thales thought the earth floated on water, Anaximenes thought the earth was flat, and Anaximander finally claimed the earth was shaped like a cylinder, and the moon was a large chariot wheel filled with fire. The phases of the moon then can be explained by the fact that the wagon wheel is at an angle. You need quite a bit of imagination for that.

The street musician Xenophanes said that the moon shines by itself and goes out every month, while his colleague Heraclitus assumed that the sun had the width of a human foot and was a rational ignition from the sea. Now, one can begin to imagine what went on at these Greek symposia when the rising alcohol level allowed thoughts to fly freely.

Finally, Parmenides went so far as to say that the earth was a sphere and that its position was in the centre of the world. Many things were asserted in those days, and sometimes they were approximately correct, most likely by chance. A few fragments of a poem by him have survived, in which '*a chariot with glowing axles and hot-running wheels*' approaches to '*the gates of the ways of Night and Day*', and whose '*changing key is kept by the goddess Dike, the mighty avenger*'.

At some point the sentence appears that there is '*whatever is is, and what is not cannot be*', from which, over two thousand years later, Mr Heidegger, who is often named as one of the most important philosophers of the 20th century, derived an entire 'philosophy of being' (Sein und Zeit). The fact that he was not exactly uncritical of the National Socialistic ideology and even spoke of a 'National Socialist Revolution' gives us a clue, which will be elaborated later.

Here now comes the time to bang one's forehead on the tabletop. Almost every standard textbook on the history of philosophy begins with this myth of the first rationally thinking scientists in world history.

'*From Mythos to Logos*', one also reads a lot, from the still mythical thinking of the East, i.e. Mesopotamia, to the enlightened rational thinking of the first Greek philosophers.

Such books about these first philosophers now fill entire libraries, most of them written in the 19th and 20th century. It is thus a rather new, and at the same time quite distorted, image of the ancient Greek philosophers. To be very clear with this, the view of the rationally thinking 'Milesian natural philosophers' dates from the late nineteenth century.

For example, the Swiss Jacob Burckhardt, whose face is still emblazoned on the thousand-franc note, wrote that only the Greeks were true scientists.

> *'Does any papyrus from Egypt or tablet from Babylon contain truths such as Anaximander's sentence: 'The earth is a body that floats freely in infinite space ... These world constructions of the Ionians from principles may have been weak guesses in themselves; what is significant and significant is that they dared to do such a thing at all?'*

Anaximander, by the way, was the one with the wagon wheel and the earth in the shape of a cylinder. Burckhardt stands for many representatives of his time and portrays the Greeks as fervent and venerable scientists who take all the trouble and expense upon themselves to attain knowledge. If one remembers the tramp Xenophanes, that what follows is 'fantasy' in its purest format.

> *'But then the sacrifices that the Greek scholar had to make were also extremely numerous and required an extremely firm moral will... Every researcher had to collect himself, which was impossible without the greatest renunciation; these people worked tremendously and were poor at the same time, in the best case not noticed by the state, without publishing rights, fees etc.'*

His 'Greek Cultural History' of 1898 is really worth reading if you want to get a picture of the distorted thinking of his time about Greek antiquity. He is representative of most of his contemporaries, and we will return to them later.

Farting philosophers

Of course, one can also go back to much older authors, such as the work of a Diogenes Laertius, who wrote his books on the 'Lives of the Eminent Philosophers' in the third century AD. Then we get an impression of why the philosophers were not taken too seriously even in their lifetime, were rather colourful 'crackers', and were probably considered the first fantasy authors in world literature. They are often uproariously funny characters who were particularly fond of beans and flatulence. Even the wondrous paths into philosophy raise some fundamental questions, and let's take a look at some of these wonderfully absurd stories.

Diogenes from Sinope, for example, the one with the barrel, was originally a banker and counterfeiter. After his own personal financial crisis, he left early for Delphi, even before he could be put in prison. From then on, he lived without money, but contentedly. As needless as a dog, he satisfied all his cravings on the street. He masturbated in public and declared: '*If it were as easy to banish hunger by rubbing the belly*'. Diogenes died at the age of ninety either from cholera or from a dog bite. Still others claim that he simply held his breath.

Crates is said to have been persuaded by Diogenes to make his land holdings available as public grazing land, and to throw what money he had into the sea. In many respects he shared the views of his colleague: '*Hunger stops love, or, if not hunger, Time', he is said to have said. 'Or, failing both these means of help, a halter'*. On the benefits of philosophy he said: '*My daily bean meal, a life without worry*'.

Metrokles, who was mentally a little 'unstable', as it seems, let out such an appallingly loud fart during his exercises in the public gymnasium that he ran home and wanted to die of starvation from shame.

Crates was asked to take care of the matter and dissuade the young man from his cruel plan. He sought out the desperate young Metrokles and explained him that it wasn't all so bad. '*gut winds need to flow freely*', he explained to him, and allowed a huge flatulence to escape himself.

So that's how Krates convinced the young man to become a philosopher: by a fart! Metrocles is said to have suffocated himself later, but whether his flatulence was involved is not known.

Zenon from Kition also came to philosophy rather by chance. While transporting purple from Phoenicia, he was shipwrecked before he even reached the port of Athens. Penniless, he went to Athens and met Crates at a bookseller's, whom he then followed and eventually became a philosopher himself. So it is possible to become a philosopher even without flatulence.

Zenon later on fell while leaving his 'school' and broke his finger. He hit the ground with his hand and quoted from the play Niobe: '*I come, I come, why dost thou call for me?*', and died on the spot through holding his breath.

All these are gloriously absurd stories that lead into philosophy, one even better than the other. One might suppose that these mentioned above were only exceptions, and the bulk of these first 'rational thinking scientists' consisted of thoroughly serious men who were striving for the knowledge of their time. So let's take a look at some of the bizarre life stories and you may judge for yourselves. The anecdotes of these men are all worth telling.

Pre-Socratic lifestyle

Thales was one of the so-called 'Seven Sages'. He was a Phoenician or a Milesian or a mixture of both. He was also a merchant, an oil mill owner, a speculator, an astronomer, an engineer, a mathematician, a seer, a statesman, a scientist, a philosopher, poor and rich, tall and short, fat and thin, a superman and an all-rounder, and probably the first exchange student in world history. He is said to have studied in Egypt and Babylon, only 'Thales's Theorem' is not from Thales, for it was known in Mesopotamia fifteen hundred years before him.

He died at seventy-eight, or at ninety, either of heatstroke in the scorching sun during a sporting event, or when he was watching the stars in the sky at night and fell into a well. He did not care, for he saw no difference between life and death. When he was once asked during his lifetime why he was not dead by then, he replied: '*because there is no difference*'.

Incidentally, another 'sage', Epimenides, the Cretan from Knossos, is said to have lain down for a bit while tending sheep and only woke up 57 years later. This quiet lifestyle could also explain his old age. He is said to have lived to be 154 or 299 years old. Others say that he only made herbal liquor, but we don't know for sure.

He is also said to have '*received from the Nymphs food of a special sort, kept it in a cow's hoof*' , and taken a little of it now and then, they say. '*But he was never seen to have had a bowel movement or to have eaten*'.

Pythagoras founded his own sect in southern Italy, believed in the transmigration of souls and resurrection. He said that '*after two hundred and seven years in Hades he has returned to the land of the living*'. His critics, however, claim that he merely hid in his mother's cellar. Moreover, his followers seemed to be firmly convinced that Pythagoras had a golden thigh, whatever that meant.

On the pleasures of Venus, he advised that one should '*practise sex in winter*', but '*only when you want to lose what strength you have*'. On the other hand, he was revered by the women of his new home town because he is said to have decreed '*that all who neglect their wives sexually would be punished*'. His sect, of course, had to follow strict rules, including such absurd regulations as '*not wiping the buttocks with oil*', '*not pissing against the sun*', and certainly '*not pissing on cut nails or hair*'.

Above all, however, he must have been fond of beans, probably not only because of the flatulence. He developed a full-blown bean phobia and strictly forbade his 'disciples' to eat them, allegedly because they resembled '*the genitals or the gates of Hades*'. It was beans that eventually became his fate.

He was eighty or ninety years old and had just been invited to Milo's house for dinner when the house was set on fire by an angry mob. The fleeing old man foolishly arrived at a bean field that he refused to cross because of his strong aversion. When his pursuers finally managed to catch up with the old man, they summarily killed him.

But it is also possible that he fled to a sanctuary and starved to death there after forty days. Or he simply got tired of living and stopped eating. The stories of his departure are numerous. It remains to add that the 'Pythagorean theorem' did not come from him, but was known long before.

Democritus, to whom we owe the name of the 'atom' could even deduce from '*the milk of a black she-goat which had produced her first kid*'. Today, people tend to make such remarks at wine tastings. And he finally also said that coitus could be compared to a temporary apoplectic stroke, with which he was probably not entirely wrong.

When he was at the end of his days, this is said to have vexed his sister very much. She wanted to attend a festival that was to last three days. A death in the family would have been a hindrance.

Democritus therefore told her to bring him warm bread every day so that he could smell it. In this way, he delayed death for three days and only died after the feast at the age of one hundred and nine. What his sister, who was probably about the same age, wanted to experience at the festival remains unclear.

Protagoras, one of the first 'sophists' who taught rhetoric in Athens, is also said to have come from Abdera, and thus brought philosophy to Athens. A good legal speech was very important, especially in the new Athenian democracy.

It was from him that the 'homo-mensura' sentence originated: '*Man is the measure of all things: of the things that are, that they are, of the things that are not, that they are not*'. The Athenians were already arguing about the content of this sentence at the time and condemned him to death.

At the very last moment he was able to save himself and escaped on a ship to Sicily. Unfortunately, he was shipwrecked and drowned shortly before reaching the island. He therefore did not live to see his colleague Empedocles jump into the Etna.

Wonderfully absurd stories entwine around these first 'philosophers', Mr Bean would certainly have had his fun. But so far there is little to be read about 'rational-physical'.

Bizarre deaths of philosophy

It would simply be too bad and unfair to leave some other philosophical highlights unmentioned before we get to the 'father of history'. While Homer's heroes die like flies on the battlefield in the cruellest possible manner, poets and thinkers have often found a very idiosyncratic way to say goodbye to the stage. One might even get the impression that there has been a secret kind of competition for the most bizarre forms of philosophical demise, and it is difficult to draw up a hit list.

Cleanthes was a philosopher who suffered from a violent inflammation of the gums. The doctors who were summoned advised him not to eat for two days. When his periodontitis improved and the doctors told him he could now eat again, Cleanthes replied that he had now become accustomed to the painless condition and did not want any more. He simply continued to starve himself and died a short time later from malnutrition, but at least without toothache.

Chrysippus was well known for hitting the bottle at the symposia. He could probably still keep his upper body under control. '*Only his legs get tipsy*' said his maid when he once again sat there rat-tight with a fixed stare, and could only fidget with his legs. Chrysippus died of a laughing fit as he watched a drunken donkey who had just decimated his fig and wine supplies.

Finally, Anaxarchus had fallen out with the tyrant of Cyprus, Nicocreon, when he was asked by him at a symposium how he liked the food. '*Magnificent*', Anaxarchos is said to have replied, '*there is only one thing missing, that the head of some satrap should be served up at table*'. Later, when he landed involuntarily in Cyprus, the tyrant had him seized, thrown into a mortar and beaten with iron pestles. '*Pound, pound the pouch containing Anaxarchus*', he is said to have shouted to the tyrant, '*ye pound not Anaxarchus*'. When Nicocreon then ordered him to cut out his tongue, Anaxarchus is said to have bitten it off himself and spat in his face before dying.

The three famous Athenian tragedians, Euripides, Sophocles and Aeschylus, probably found their inspiration in the philosophers. Euripides is said to have been mauled by dogs when he followed the Macedonian king Archelaus to Pella, and Sophocles died in the same year as his fellow poet when he choked on a grape.

The coup, however, was landed by the eldest of the three. Aeschylus was prophesied to be killed by a stone. Fearing that the house above him would collapse, he therefore went to an open field. Unfortunately, an eagle, which had previously caught a turtle, happened to be circling above his head, looking for a way to break open its shell. The eagle mistook the old poet's bald skull in the open field for a blank stone, took accurate aim and brought its turtle down unerringly on his fontanel from a lofty height. Whether the turtle survived has not been passed on, but the poet did not. Death by turtle. You have to come up with that first.

But bizarre deaths still happen today. More than two thousand years later, Jacques LeFevrier from France did not want to leave anything to chance in his intended suicide and became the winner of the 1999 Darwin Awards with his story.

He stood on a high cliff and hung a rope around his neck, which he tied to a nearby rock. In addition, he drank poison and set fire to his clothes. He also tried to shoot himself with a pistol on his way down from the cliff.

So he jumped off the cliff, missed when shooting and hit the rope instead. This caused him to fall into the floods below, which immediately extinguished the flames. As he swallowed water, he threw up and immediately got rid of the poison.

A friendly fisherman pulled him out of the water and took him to a nearby hospital. There, he finally died of hypothermia.

So let's close the round of unbelievable deaths here and continue with our story. You may not have noticed, but a good two hundred years have passed since Thales and Cyrus, and the Persians are said to have visited Athens twice, tells us Herodotus.

It is time, therefore, to take a closer look at this 'Father of History', whom we had already met in Egypt. It will now become interesting for all the followers of the faction who believe the heroic battles of the Greeks at Marathon and Thermopylae against the evil Persians, which are written in our history books.

Herodotus in Bodenwerder

Herodotus' 'Histories' are one of the first, at times screamingly funny, travel descriptions in literary history, mixed with historical accounts, ancient myths and legends, stories experienced or allegedly experienced, and often depictions of utterly abstruse rituals across all the then known lands. Finally, the story ends in the grandiose descriptions of the overwhelming Persian attacks at Marathon and Thermopylae against the vastly inferior yet heroic, noble Athenians and Spartans. His audience had to be kept happy, after all, and they paid well.

Herodotus story begins first in Lydia, with that king Croesus whom we still know today as an indescribably rich man. It was the country where the game of dice was invented, where all women prostituted themselves before their marriage, and chose their husband on their own. By Greek standards, a veritable Sodom and Gomorrah.

Before Croesus now moves against the advancing Persians, he gets his famous oracle saying: '*if you move against the Persians, you destroy a great empire*'. What the oracle meant, however, was his own, but oracles are like that. He could only be defeated by a trick. The Persians simply continued to fight in winter, while the Lydians knew what was proper and went home when it was getting cold, preferring to sit in front of the warming hearth instead of slashing skulls.

Finally, Herodotus tells the story of how Croesus came to power and why he had to lose, and we are now witnessing the first 'peeping tom' in world literature.

Croesus' great-great-great-grandfather was Gyges, this king who had allegedly made a fortune by hiring out mercenaries to Egypt, and shortly afterwards asked Ashurbanipal for help himself.

Gyges, however, was in the beginning only an advisor to King Candaules, whom obviously no one believed how beautiful his wife was. '*I see thou dost not credit what I tell thee of my lady's loveliness*', Candaules said to his puzzled adviser, '*Wouldst thou have me behold my mistress when she is naked?*'. Gyges was told to hide behind the door while his wife undressed in front of the king and to watch secretly and without being caught.

These kind of thing always go wrong, and already the ancient Greeks knew that very well. Of course Gyges wife found out what was going on, and so, a little later, the exposed wife gave Gyges, who was looking down in shame, the choice of either dying himself or stabbing her husband to death and taking his place on the throne. She was not only beautiful, but also not stupid, for what could one do with a man who brought the voyeurs into his own house.

Gyges did not have to think twice, took up his dagger and became the new king. But the oracle at Delphi had prophesied that his deed would be atoned for in five generations. And Croesus was his great-great-great-grandson.

Incidentally, we find a modified version of the story of Gyges later in the philosopher Plato's 'Politeia', a book in which the philosopher wants to found a slightly 'fascistoid' guardian state. Here, Gyges comes across the corpse of a giant in a small cave that he discovers purely by chance, and this giant has a golden ring on his finger, which he pulls off. This ring, once he had put it on and twisted it, amazingly made the wearer invisible. If you think you can find some parallels to nowadays stories, you might probably want to consider that Mr Tolkien could have read these old works and used them in his books about the world of the hobbits in his 'Lord of the rings'.

But come back to Herodotus. The Persian Wars, for which he is best known, exist only in Greek sources, and apart from Herodotus' Histories there is only one tragedy that tells of them, written by the same Aeschylus who had the turtle dropped on his head.
He had performed his play 'The Persians' in Athens about forty years before Herodotus. Real sources are rather limited, as you may see, but nonetheless the Persian wars are still mentioned in almost all history books as one of the great touring points of western civilization. So let's take a very brief look at the two great epic battles that Homer describes in his book and which are still being tought and burned into the brains of educated people and do some calculation. Very briefly, so that you can see how absurd these stories are.

According to Herodotus, six hundred triremes with a crew of two hundred men each, landed at

Marathon, which makes about one hundred and twenty thousand Persians against some ten thousand Greeks. At the end of the battle six thousand four hundred Persians were killed and a total of seven Persian ships are captured. If you want to believe that, go ahead. But!

One hundred and twenty thousand soldiers would have covered the entire area with fifty tons of excrement and four hundred thousand litres of urine in the three days before the alleged battle. No spade in the Bible would have helped, the attacking Athenians would simply have been stuck up to their necks in 'Heraclitean' excrements, and we haven't even included all the supply troops that would have been needed to feed one hundred and twenty thousand Persian soldiers.

The story becomes even more beautiful with the second Persian attack several years later, with two million six hundred and forty-one thousand six hundred and ten men, one thousand two hundred and seven warships and three thousand transport ships. This results in a ship convoy well over one hundred kilometres long. The legendary ship bridge over the Bosporus could have been spared, apart from the fact that there would have been no trees left standing in the entire eastern Mediterranean.

The soldiers alone would have polluted their environment with three hundred tons of excrement and two and a half million litres of urine every day, not counting the one hundred thousand horses, the huge herds of cattle for slaughter, together with the cattle breeders and butchers, the craftsmen and bakers and everything they needed, the escorts, women and children, who were always with them, the jugglers and actors for the entertainment in between, and the crowds of toy boys and prostitutes, who accompanied this cortege by the tens of thousands and ensured a contented, happy sleep for their clientele. A troop that Herodotus estimates to be 'no less numerous, indeed even more in number than the actual army'. That would be a total of six hundred tons of feaces and five million litres of urine, every day!

Half the Orient, more than five million people, would have been on their way to Athens. An illustrious bunch of happily pissing and pooping creatures. The Persians would not have had to fight at all. The trail of faecal devastation would have turned whole swathes of land and regions into manure fields and cesspits.

Logistically, these masses would never have been able to push their way through the pass at Thermopylae, at least not without wading through metre-high floods of shit, while the ships in the naval battle at Artemision would have carried out their manoeuvres in a huge septic tank. But beautiful stories they are nonetheless, the ones about the three hundred Spartans and their king Leonidas.

Herodotus was a storyteller and his stories were brilliant. The fund of stories in Herodotus' 'Histories' is almost immeasurable. But to call him the 'Father of History' would be a bit of an exaggeration, and what did anyone want to do with historiography back then? There were no universities, not schools, and not even any interest in history as we know it today. The subject of 'history' only appeared in the early nineteenth century, around the time the University of Göttingen was founded.

The cities of antiquity were tiny by today's standards. With five thousand men you were already a big city, and even Athens probably never had more than forty thousand inhabitants. Everyone knew everyone else, and life took place on the streets.

If a 'philosopher' like Xenophanes ever came by, he had to reveal his 'works' in the marketplace, right next to the fruit seller and the barber surgeon. With a bit of luck, he was even invited by a rich fellow citizen to a symposium to give his best there with full catering. Who loves not woman, wine and song, will be a fool his whole life long, and Herodotus does not seem to have been an idiot. Fancy a symposium?

Greek symposium

Let us take part in such a drinking bout, at which the housewife is of course not to be found. But there is talk of one or two flute players, a few prostitutes, or even a catamite who took care of the guests. Tonight's theme is Egypt, and everyone is dressed up and styled accordingly, including the belly-dancing troupe with the flute players and the two catamites. There is plenty to eat and drink, the bellies are full, liver and kidneys are running at full speed. Most of the guests are already more than tipsy, lolling on their couches and listening to the words that are coming. Curtain up, Herodotus enters the stage, and after a few introductory words, the 'Father of History' begins his report, first about the Egyptian animal world:

'*The catching of crocodiles is done in many ways*', he recites. '*They bait a hook with a chine of pork and let the meat be carried out into the middle of the stream, while the hunter upon the bank holds a living pig, which he belabours. The crocodile hears its cries, and making for the sound, encounters the pork, which he instantly swallows down. The men on the shore haul, and when they have got him to land, the first thing the hunter does is to plaster his eyes with wax. This once accomplished, the animal is despatched with ease, otherwise you are in great trouble*', recites Herodotus.

Egyptian cats displayed particularly strange behavioural anomalies during a fire, Herodotus tells his audience. '*The inhabitants allow the fire to rage as it pleases, while they stand about at intervals and watch these animals, which, slipping by the men or else leaping over them, rush headlong into the flames. When this happens, the Egyptians are in deep affliction.*'

The first images of suicidal cats buzz through the minds of the listeners. But Herodotus continues calmly, almost bored: '*If a cat dies in a private house by a natural death, all the inmates of the house shave their eyebrows;on the death of a dog they shave the head and the whole of the body*'. The audience's imagination is slowly stirred, the first laughs are heard, the audience is ready for more. If you think Herodotus somehow had the Egyptians on the kicker, well, he's just getting warmed up now.

'*The way of life of the Egyptians is this*', he recites, '*For three successive days in each month they purge the body by means of emetics and clysters, which is done out of a regard for their health*'. Unpleasant pictures are running through the minds of the audience, and rectally inserted enemas take on plastic forms in it, while the first tears start to well up in some of the guests. Others hold their full bellies while a tender playmate lets out a light fart with laughter. '*Gut winds need to flow freely*', Crates agrees, the philosopher from the next table.

When a respected member of the household dies, Herodotus continues, '*all the women in the household cover their heads or faces with faeces, leave the corpse in the house and walk through the town with their breasts exposed and beating themselves*', Herodotus continues calmly, while some of the visitors have already fallen off their couches and are rolling on the floor with belly-aching laughter.

'*All the female relatives join them and do the same*', he comments calmly. '*The men also beat themselves and have their robes tied under their chests*'. The vivid fantasies of some attendees show faeces-covered, bare-breasted women running through the narrow streets of Naucratis, pursued by a pack of slavering men with their robes raised and their penises erected. A few soft squeaks indicate that some of the guests are now in acute respiratory distress. Gasping for breath sets in. '*After this we proceed to embalm the corpse*'.

The whole show goes on for hours, and what the Egyptians now do with their dead corpses is something, that should rather be read by oneself. But if you ever want to pick up an entertaining 'history book', then this is the one. Herodotus' 'Histories' are full of such absurd stories, and it is up to everyone to call him the 'Father of History'.

But let us now return to our actual history. What is known of the 'philosophers' before Socrates is rather doubtful. The idea of 'purely rational scientists' springs from nineteenth-century fantasies, and is still vehemently held today, in particular in Germany. We will see later where this comes from, and how this attitude was formed. Now we come to two philosophers whose texts and views have been preserved, and amazingly, we frequently find their ideas and conceptions even today. Let's go to Athens and start getting a bit more serious.

Athenian triumvirate

Socrates was the first 'Athenian' philosopher, and he probably got on his fellow men's nerves so much that he was put on trial in 399 BC. He left nothing in writing, and his students gave different accounts of him.

Only a few took him seriously, as we can see from the words of his contemporary comedian writer Aristophanes and his work 'The Clouds'. When asked whether a mosquito buzzed through its proboscis or through its anus, Socrates replied:

> *'The mosquito's intestine is narrow and that air is forced through this constricted space leading up to the abdomen, at which point the arse, an orifice attached to a narrow tube, emits a sound under the pressure of the gas'.*

> *'The mosquito's arse is a trumpet'*, replied his new student, full of delight. *'Thrice happy Socrates! He is marvelously blessed with gut instincts. A man with such a knowledge of the mosquito's insides would definitely get off easily if he was on trial'*

I already told you that ancient Greeks and flatulences form a bizarre unity. In any case, Socrates seems to have taken it with humour. During the performance of the play he stood up and presented himself to the audience, so that everyone could see who was being paraded. When he was actually on trial a little later, he was sentenced to death and had to drink the poisonous cup of hemlock. The intestinal knowledge of the mosquito was of no use to him at all.

His circle of students must have been quite illustrious. They included Xenophon, the one who was on his way from Babylon to Mosul with his ten thousand Greeks; Alcibiades, the prototype of an unscrupulous political turncoat, who was later accused of cutting off the willies of all the statues of Hermen on the road to the harbour; and Plato, whom we will come to know in a moment. The only one who seemed a little out of the ordinary was the young Phadeo, who had to earn his money as a catamite in an Athenian brothel. What became of him, however, remains just as hidden as the question of whether this pupilage of Socrates really corresponds to historical truth. Nevertheless, the stories are and remain unquestionably ingenious.

Only with Plato and Aristotle we do finally have two philosophers of whom at least some works have survived and who really had a deep influence on western thinking.

Plato was a filthy rich Athenian aristocrat who pulled out all the stops to get his name in lights. He wrote of himself in the third person and gave himself the name Socrates in his works, who now delivered page-long monologues at the symposia. It is these writings that have a strong influence on our image of Socrates today.

If you read Plato's 'Politeia' today, for example, associations of a police state, political censorship and genetic breeding programmes will pop into ones head at some point. Plato has his Socrates construct an authoritarian 'ideal state' that assigns every shepherd, every farmer, every craftsman, every 'guardian' and every philosopher to their natural and immovable place in society. The gods have put gold or silver up the backsides of the upper social classes, the watchmen and philosophers, whereas the 'souls' of the lower classes consist only of base materials such as copper or iron.

And so that nothing mixes, each stratum keeps to itself. He who was born stupid remained stupid, even if one tries to explain something to him, Plato thought. Iron and copper remain iron and copper, as he explained in his 'Allegory of the Cave'.

The 'capable and perfect guardians' of this Politeia are subject to a breeding programme. '*These women must belong to all men together*', Plato writes, '*none may be with any alone, and likewise the children are common. Neither the father knows his child, nor the child his father*'. His opinion about women was probably not too high, but that's just a guess.

At the head of this 'ideal state' is, of course, the wisest of all philosophers, and you can imagine who Plato had in mind. Three times he tried to realise his ideas in Sicily. Time and again he was arrested, and could only escape at the last minute. About two and a half thousand years were to pass before the unsuccessful postcard artist Addi H. from Braunau and his followers put similar delusions into practice.

Plato's writings reflected the ideas of the 'upper class' at a time, when costly, paid mercenary armies had become the norm. His unpaid 'guards' were as illusory as the 'incorruptible' philosopher-ruler and the curtailment of political participation in the then 'democratic' Athens.

He writes at a time when the idea of an immortal soul was slowly gaining ground in society, which was also evident in various mystery cults. Presumably, these ideas originally came from the Persian highlands in what is now Iran, from where they spread to India in the east and to the Greek cities in the west.

Until then, the Greek view had been that life ended with death and that there was endless boredom in the underworld. Now a new view was slowly gaining ground that life somehow continued after death. Accordingly, in his 'Phaedo', Plato conceived of an immortal soul that lived on after death and a mortal body that decayed after death, which he also referred to again and again in other writings.

In 'Timaeus', one of his late works, he even speaks of a kind of transmigration of the soul. He went so far as to say that if a man lived a bad life, he would be reborn as a woman for punishment. Somehow, it seems, he really had a serious problem with women.

These ideas, however, were further developed over the next centuries, and became the basic element of Christian faith and the Catholic Church. The idea of an 'afterlife', of a 'life after death', of a separation of 'body and mind', of 'material and immaterial', or of 'heart and soul' have their origin here, and still determine the thinking of our time. The church father Augustine in particular brought many elements of this doctrine into the Christian ideas, including the idea of the four elements 'fire, water, earth, air', which were developed in antiquity and by Plato.

With the advent of Christianity, people finally had a belief in a single God, combined with the ideas of the afterlife, which had largely developed in Greece. Many of the religious concepts probably originated in the ancient myths of Mesopotamia, and some ancient philosophical writings from Athens. However, it is almost impossible to convince someone of a 'Greek-Assyrian' or even 'Persian culture', that form the backbone of western actual thinking.

But let's continue in the text and come to the number three. Aristotle from Stagira was a very different character, and in many ways the exact opposite of Plato. He was a logical thinker and must have had the charm of a pedantic librarian.

He collected, archived and noted everything he could get his hands on, be it stones, beetles, plants and the constitutional texts of Greek city states. He catalogued and grouped words, languages, ideas, knowledge and ethics.

Everything he found, he put in the appropriate drawers, and thereby created an order of everything that was wonderfully attractive to so many people.

Immanuel Kant from Königsberg said of himself some two thousand years later, that he was probably the only one who understood the old Stagiraer, because he too tried to put everything into individual drawers, only he called them categories.

And if you put everything nicely into drawers, you create order, and order is the half of your life, a German saying says. So let's only hope that the other half is a bid more interesting.

Of course, Aristotle also had a drawer for humans. He first distinguished between living beings that lived individually, and those that lived in groups. With the latter, there were living beings that simply lived together in a heap, while others organised themselves. And those living beings that lived together in groups and organised themselves he called 'political beings', which included bees, ants and cranes as well as humans. So someone who calls himself a 'political being' or 'zoon politicon' today is probably something like an ant or a crane.

Aristotle probably preferred reasonable and logically thinking people, because that is how he defined them. In any case, the difference between humans and animals is 'reason', Aristotle said. If this idea had prevailed, the world would probably look different today, but it would certainly not be as entertaining.

In any case, the geocentric view of the world that Aristotle advocated in his writings would prove to have serious consequences, even if he was completely in line with the views of the time.

> *'Heavy bodies move towards the centre of the earth, light and fire move in the opposite direction to the heavy. The earth must therefore be at the centre of the universe, and motionless. An object thrown vertically upwards would fall back to the same point, even if the force threw it upwards indefinitely. That the earth does not move and is not outside the centre is clear from what has been said'.*

Whole generations were to work on this image, because it determined the later world view of the Catholic Church, which elevated these views to dogma.

The idea of his order of things was simply too beautiful. It fitted into the concept that everything had its regular course.

Aristotle's writings, however, were considered lost for a long time and only caused a sensation in the Middle Ages when they were slowly rediscovered. His writings had survived in the Arab countries. Science and literature were flourishing there, and medieval Europe was far behind in all aspects.

It was only through contact with the Arab countries in Spain, southern Italy and the eastern Mediterranean that Aristotle's ideas came back to Europe. And while they were at it, they also imported the Arabic numbers that we use today, arithmetic, the algorithm, calculating with the number 'zero', and many other things, such as eating with a knife and fork and, of course, coffee.

Aristotle's writings were soon considered as an 'iron law', and it was simply assumed that he had already explored everything that was to explore. Even today, we associate him with concepts such as 'matter', 'category', or 'theory and practice'. His logic, his way of reasoning, his stereotype thinking and categorizing, and his geocentric view of the world soon found their way into the Catholic Church and the universities.

With Aristotle we finally leave Greece and the whole of antiquity. We have seen where some of the very old ideas come from that we still adhere to today. They formed a view of the world that lasted for centuries and can still be found today in many areas.

It is time to turn to the Enlightenment and see what has become of it. We can safely leave the rest of antiquity and the Middle Ages behind. Plato's ideas were firmly anchored in the Christian faith, and what happened to Aristotle's thinking we will see in a moment.

However, the idea that Greek philosophy was also the beginning of 'rational-physical science' is a fairly recent myth, developed towards the end of the nineteenth century. So it is time to return to the present, or rather to the beginning of the Enlightenment. Let's see what has become of all those ideas, and where the view that the Greeks had already thought everything that could be thought came from.

On the journey, I'll tell them the story of Hermann of Reichenau, also called 'the Lame', whom you may not know in person, but who did something very interesting that we still benefit from every day. So, back to the future, and to the place where the Enlightenment began....

Newer Stories

Hermann der Lame
Confessions of a late riser
The story of the new thinking
Falling Stones
Heaven on earth
Let there be light
Royal droppings
I stink therefore I am
Bouillon Rectal
Lac du Annecy
Story of the Haute Cuisine
Interesting Times

Hermann the Lame

On our journey, we can once consider the question of how long we are actually calculating with the terms 'before' and 'after' Christ.

The spontaneous answer is usually: 'for about two thousand years'. But quite honestly, as nice as the birth of such a little mucky pup is, no one starts a new era with it. With the first child, many young parents can still claim that, but wait until the second comes along.

This is where Hermann of Reichenau, also called 'The Lame' comes into play, the Steven Hawkins of the early Middle Ages. When Charlemagne sat in Aachen around 800 AD, he must have noticed that his people were in urgent need of some education. They were, to say it nicely, profoundly 'illiterate'.

Most of the writings of antiquity were unknown in north-western Europe, hardly anyone could read or write, and even Charles had a hard time with it. Aachen, like the entire empire of the Franks, was an educational desert. Often, the dusty shelves of the rare libraries contained only a poor Bible and the odd local chronicle, and even these were useless to the vast majority of the population. The life of a librarian was thus quite contemplative.

So Charles initiated an educational programme, which consisted first of all of acquiring material. He relied mainly on the Catholic Church and its monasteries, which already had a certain infrastructure. The Church not only brought people who could read and write, it also imported its own world view, the foundations of which we have just heard about. It was the time when the Christianisation of Europe was in full swing.

Hermann of Reichenau came to the Benedictine monastery in Reichenau on Lake Constance around 1020 AD. He suffered from lateral sclerosis, and had himself carried around the monastery tied to a portable saddle. Like his British colleague almost a thousand years later, Hermann was busy with the latest astronomical equipment he could get his hands on. In his case it was an 'astrolabe' from Arabia. He was interested in whether and how a clear determination of time was feasible.

Of course, this Hermann was not only a scientist, but also a historian, writer and musician. A true polymath. But in his time, one did not need four studies and thirty years of education to become one. There were no schools or universities; the monasteries took over these functions. Admittedly, there wasn't that much to study yet either.

In any case, the monasteries started copying everything they could get their hands on. Some documents leaked over the Alps from Italy, some from the still Christian Constantinople, and most of the information came from Moorish Spain.

The first 'universities' were founded, and very gradually a first 'basic knowledge' spread, strongly influenced by the now newly discovered writings of the ancient philosopher Aristotle, that were preserved and formed part of the Arabian culture.

In any case, Hermann was the first author to write a detailed, continuous chronicle since the birth of Christ, always accompanied with the notation 'Anno Domini', the year of the Lord.

Until then, completely different terms had been in circulation. 'In the year the wheat fell', or 'the year my neighbour's horse kicked me', were perfectly common year designations. They are still in use today, like 'the summer that was so hot' or 'Christmas when there was so much snow', but people prefer to use other terms for documentation purposes.

The use of the previous chronicles according to ruler dates, such as 'in the fifth year of Charlemagne', also proved difficult. Comparing dates was complicated, and one had to have a lot of chronicles in one's head in order to know when, what and where something happened. And, of course, it was even more difficult to talk about future events, because one could never know how long the current ruler would remain in office. Obviously, planning years ahead had its pitfalls.

It was to take several more centuries before Hermann's division with 'BC' and 'AD' finally prevailed. But with Herrmann we have the first recorded chronicler who used a consistent time indication with 'Anno Domini'.

In Britain a dating method based on the year of reign of the respective king remained in place until 1962, at least for the Acts of the British Parliament. Until then, every student had to learn the names and dates of all kings by heart and in the correct order.

We have already reached the end of our journey through space and time, and finally arrived at the place where the 'Age of Enlightenment' decisively began. Everybody out, take your coats on, it's getting cold outside. Welcome to ... Ulm!

Confessions of a late riser

We begin our story in a small but well-heated cabinet in the winter of 1619. It is late morning and a young French soldier is just waking up in his bed, probably wondering what the hell he is doing here.

A few weeks ago he had joined Duke Maximilian of Bavaria to take part in the religious wars that had recently broken out. Bavaria (Bayern) was still spelled with an 'i' back then. He didn't really care who paid his pay, Protestants or Catholics, because this war wasn't really about religious convictions. He had previously served on the Protestant side, then travelled through Denmark and the German lands until he finally landed here in Bavaria.

However, the battlefields were now so soggy in the winter that the soldiers had no choice but to either drink themselves pointlessly stupid to Bavarian beer or otherwise kill time.

The young Frenchman was not without means and had received a fairly solid education at a Jesuit college in La Flèche in France. However, he was never a really good pupil. He never really got on with the thinking of his teachers. Three years ago, at the age of just twenty, he had finished his law studies and then started travelling instead of taking up a job in the civil service, as was generally the case.

The world of René Descartes, so was the name of the young soldier, was really weird. While the whole world had recently been discovered and merchant ships were now sailing all the world's oceans, people were at the same time increasingly believing in magical powers and the devil, in a mystical environment full of demons, in astrology and alchemy, in dark sorcery, and above all in witchcraft. Even in Ulm, witch hunts were not uncommon, and throughout the 'Reich' this delusion was just heading for its sad climax, to which thousands of people were to fall victim. There seemed to be no end to the hysteria and belief in the supernatural, and in the midst of this madness, a religious war was taking place in which the young Frenchman was involved.

Descartes probably faced the same problem as many people today, some four hundred years later. So many absurd stories were being told, so many foolish believes were circulating, and so much stupid stuff was being believed that eventually one no longer knew oneself whom one could trust at all, or what one should believe at all.

Perhaps it was precisely this mixture and the gullibility of his fellow men that got on the young Frenchman's nerves so badly, that one late winter morning, in his warm bed in Ulm, he asked himself how he could actually put an end to all this nonsense in this world and gain truly secure knowledge.

He was certainly not aware that the thoughts he put down on paper during those days would one day become one of the central documents of the Enlightenment. But one thing was clear to him: '*For to be possessed of a vigorous mind is not enough*', he wrote in his 'Discourse on the Method of Rightly Conducting One's Reason and of Seeking Truth in the Sciences. '*The prime requisite is rightly to apply it*'.

It is not enough, therefore, to have a mind alone; whoever possesses this divine gift should also make the best use of it. And that in turn meant countering all the absurd stories and beliefs with reasonable doubt. So Descartes, at just twenty-three years of age, formulated four 'precepts' that he would follow in the future:

> *The first was never to accept anything for true which I did not clearly know to be such.*
> *The second, to divide each of the difficulties under examination into as many parts as possible, and as might be necessary for its adequate solution.*
> *The third, to conduct my thoughts in such order that, by commencing with objects the simplest and easiest to know, I might ascend by little and little to the knowledge of the more complex.*
> *And the last, in every case to make enumerations so complete, and reviews so general, that I might be assured that nothing was omitted.*

Descartes did nothing but to ask for the 'why', the cause, why the world is the way it is. He was looking for the reason of a thing, he was looking for the 'primordial' thing. And he was thus also asking about the consequences that resulted from it, that is, about the 'effect'. So his whole approach is nothing other than the rational thinking of 'cause and effect'.

In order not to completely despair of his own rules and really have to question everything and everyone, he of course first needed a stable basis, and he proceeded quite pragmatically. Instead of immediately throwing all one's previous principles and convictions overboard, or as he put it, completely demolishing the house one lives in and only then rebuilding it, it would be better to consider renovating the individual rooms step by step.

The anchor that was to give one support in the floods of scepticism, or the foundation on which one could build one's house, was one's own mind. So he who doubted his own mind had a problem. His method was to use the mind correctly, but not to doubt it. And that's where his famous sentence came from:

'*Je pense, donc je suis*' - I think, therefore I am.

There is also a little anecdote about this sentence: When Descartes wanted to have dinner in a small guesthouse in Ulm, he sat down at a table and looked at the menu with the dish of the day. '*May I bring you something to eat?*' the owner of the inn asked him. '*With pleasure,*' Descartes replied. '*And would you like something to drink with it?*' asked the owner, who was already setting about filling the plate in the kitchen. '*I don't think*', Descartes answered him, vanished into a cloud of logic and was no more.

The wonderful thing about Descartes' four precepts now was that they could be applied to any field. Now that he was already using his brain, he assumed, on the basis of purely logical and rational observations of 'cause and effect', that the blood must circulate in the body. Not only did he thus contradict the common view and the latest medical research of his time, which assumed that blood was constantly being formed anew in the liver, but he had thus also explained the blood circulation and the essential functions of heart and lungs, veins and arteries in the human body decades before William Harvey. It is always amazing to see what a good nap is for.

His new method could be applied in mathematics, algebra, and physics as well as in philosophy or any other science. '*What satisfied me most in this method was that by it I was sure to use my mind in everything, if not perfectly, at least as well as it was in my power*'.

Not only to carry one's brain through the world as a massive matter under the fontanel, but also to actually make use of this organ, is probably one of those timeless requests that should always be given some emphasis in every epoch.

When Descartes finally decided to use his own mind in his winter quarters, it must have dawned on him quite soon that this war was not for him and he had better get the hell out of there. Over the next few years, he travelled all over Europe and never stayed in one place for long.

The Thirty Years' War did not end until 1648. In England, a revolution the following year led to the execution of the king, while in France the Huguenots were persecuted and expelled. The philosopher, now already in his fifties, was not doomed by religious disputes, however, but by a twenty-four-year-old, educated woman in the form of Queen Christina of Sweden, who invited him to her court in Stockholm.

Young Christina, unfortunately, and quite contrary to Mr Descartes' custom, had the silly habit of receiving her guests before sunrise and riding out with them if necessary, which was something of a challenge to his health in wintry Sweden.

Descartes, with his preference for heated rooms and long sleeps, endured this ordeal for a whole two months before taking his leave and dying of pneumonia. 'Early to bed and early to rise makes a man healthy, wealthy, and wise', a saying says – and sometimes extremely dead, one might add.

Certainly, it was not his intention to oppose the Catholic Church. Nevertheless, in 1663, a few years after his death, his works were placed on the Index of Forbidden Books. An unmistakable guarantee that his works were actually read and appreciated. All the more reason, then, to take a closer look at the thinking of his time.

The story of the new thinking

At about the same time as Descartes wrote his 'Disourse on the Method', David Herlitz wrote his 'Discourse on the Comet', in which he interpreted celestial phenomena that were occurring frequently at that time. For him, everything pointed to the fact that the end of the world was approaching, and that the Lord would finally put an end to the ungodly turmoil of the unbelievers, a world full of '*abominable fornication, whoredom, incest, and illegitimate cohabitation*'.

He was convinced that the current world was a Sodom and Gomorrah, in which the old authority of the sovereigns now also was opposed. He speculated that these divine signs of wrath now foretold great droughts and storm winds, foul and poisonous vapours, disease, pestilence and war, and of course he referred also to Aristotle.

There was not the slightest trace of science and rational thinking to be observed. The whole world view of the time was strongly influenced by the Church and, lo and behold, by Aristotle, or 'Aristotelianism', whose writings were by now well known in Europe.

Descartes himself was trained by representatives of this strict world view, which divided the world into pigeonholes and celestial spheres. Above was the sphere of fire, below that the spheres of air, water and finally the earth. Outside these spheres existed the divine ether, in which the celestial bodies orbit the world in perfect because divine circles, and did not follow earthly laws. Also the Creator was to be found there in heaven, contemplating his work and guiding the destinies of humanity. That was the thinking at the time.

When it came to the question of secure knowledge, the main question was, with Aristotle, which of the drawers it would fit into. Roughly speaking, one asked for the: 'WHAT is it?' and looked for the appropriate drawer.

Since there was not always agreement, of course, a strictly defined argumentation technique was needed in the upcoming debates. After all, they were only looking for the right drawer; Aristotle had already taken care of the knowledge. To give the whole thing a nice name, the word 'scholasticism' was chosen for this technique. So, no witchcraft at all.

The method was a kind of derivation from something big to something small, like the following example: '*All men wear ties, Socrates is a man, Socrates wears a tie*'. The crucial thing was that it was not questioned whether men really had to wear ties. Nor was it asked why men wore ties. What was important was that, based on the premise '*all men wear ties*', the reasoning was correct and finally led to '*Socrates wears a tie*'. Of course, one can also go through the whole thing with women and lipstick or any other formality of which one claims 'that's how it's done'. So you still encounter this thinking today. If you don't believe it, try walking naked through a department store.

That means, science is above all the following of rules based on premises that are not doubted or questioned. Even back then, it was clear to everyone that this kind of argumentation was used to play tricks, such as '*all donkeys pee standing up, Socrates pees standing up, Socrates is a donkey'*. The correct translation should actually be: All donkeys pee standing up, Socrates is a donkey, Socrates pees standing up. Whether Socrates was a donkey or the donkey was called Socrates is then entirely in the eye of the beholder.

Resistance to this kind of teaching arose early on. As early as the fourteenth and fifteenth centuries, scholasticism was, for Francesco Petrarch and Erasmus of Rotterdam, a 'book learning' whose 'artful argumentation' fixated too much on the teachings of Aristotle, and which was now represented primarily by the Church.

Boccaccio's 'Decamerone' also mocked the bigotry and spiritual unworldliness of the Roman Catholic Church of the time as early as the fourteenth century. He tells the story of the young Masetto, who tricked himself into working as a supposedly mute gardener in a women's monastery. When Masetto returns to his village after years of fruitful work, during which he had made happy the entire female staff, including their abbess, he is the progenitor of a whole flock of pious convent children.

But let us return to our story. For a long time, scholasticism remained the only recognised method of teaching at the established universities of Europe, where mainly theology, law and medicine were taught. With Descartes now, doubt entered into sciences, and the difference of his 'method' from the hitherto common approach was enormous.

With Descartes, it is now a question of what can I know, how can I know it and, above all, why are things the way they are. It was no longer just about 'WHAT is it', but about 'WHY is it'. Descartes breaks down a problem into many individual steps, which he solves one by one. He comes from smaller individual results to a larger overall result, whereas until then people argued just the other way round, arguing from something big to something small. It was nothing but the complete reversal of old way of thinking.

Falling Stones

Many problems arose from the more recent observations that could not be reconciled with previous knowledge. According to ancient thinking, the world consisted of the four elements earth, water, fire and air. Consequently, every object is drawn to where it belongs. So every body has a natural destination, everything belonged in its drawer, and Aristotle had given that order long before.

A stone, for example, is made of the element earth and falls to the ground because that is where it belongs. It falls directly towards the centre of the earth. Fire, on the other hand, rises upwards, because above is the sphere of fire. According to ancient thinking, the stone did exactly what it was meant to do. The stone is from the element earth. Earth belongs to earth, and the stone followed its destiny. This ancient view was aligned with a purpose, a destiny, or a meaning. In the pervasive religious ideas, everything had to serve a higher purpose, follow a divine plan that had to be deciphered. Everything was oriented towards an ultimate goal. This was the old thinking of 'meaning and purpose'.

This, of course, led to some rather comical views today. For example, a bird, because it can fly, is made of the element air. A cannonball, on the other hand, is made of the element earth, and its trajectory corresponds roughly to that of a triangle. The shot initially catapults the ball in a certain direction. Once this energy is used up, the movement stops and the ball falls almost vertically to the ground, where it belongs. A movement is therefore only possible as long as there is a cause for the movement. We still know corresponding drawings from the history books.

But, a puck on an ice hockey field simply glides on without any further impulse and does not stop abruptly. Representatives of the old school of thought now explained this phenomenon by the fact that a swirl forms behind the puck. This turbulence forms a separate cause of movement that carries the puck on even after the original impulse has ended. You can also make it complicated when it is actually quite simple.

Galileo Galilei, another contemporary of Descartes, now brought a completely different reasoning. Galileo claimed that a body maintains the direction of its motion until it is stopped or redirected by another force.

The consequence was that it was no longer necessary to explain why the puck kept moving on the ice, but why it stopped moving. So why doesn't the puck just keep sliding on the ice endlessly.

The falling of the stone on the floor was no longer a 'natural characteristic' for him. The floor was also no longer the 'natural destination' of the stone. Now the question was 'why' the stone falls, the question of the cause, of a certain force that pulls the stone from its original position in the air towards the earth. It was the thinking of 'cause and effect'.

For us today, this is much more understandable if we imagine an astronaut in zero gravity on his space station. If this astronaut 'drops' a stone from his hand in zero gravity, the stone remains nailed to its place. It does not fall. It remains in the place where it was released. On Earth, however, the same stone inevitably falls to the ground. So Galileo now asks about the force behind it. What force exists on Earth, but not in zero gravity.

It is this the beginning of the dispute between Aristotle and Descartes, between old and new thinking, between 'meaning and purpose' and 'cause and effect'. It is precisely this confrontation that we encounter to this day. It is the whole pivot of the Enlightenment.

Heaven on Earth

Galileo's problem, however, was that he could not explain why the moon circles around the earth. If a body maintains its direction, why does the moon rotate in circles around the earth and does not fly out into space? A question that was finally answered by Isaac Newton some fifty years later. So to round up the picture of the new thinking, we need to talk about him for a moment.

Newton was looking for the force that kept the moon in its orbit around the earth. His 'Principia Mathematica', which appeared in 1687, was not originally designed to challenge the Christian faith. However, Newton was able to show that the force that causes a stone to fall to the ground on Earth is the same force that keeps the Moon in its orbit. He called this force gravitation. In the absence of gravity, the stone on Earth would simply 'hang' in the air, and in the absence of gravity, the Moon would vanish straight out into space.

Many people know Newton's law of universal gravitation from the story in in which Newton was sitting under an apple tree one day and suddenly an apple fell on his head. It is said that he understood at that moment that the forces on earth and the forces in heaven are the same. Well, Newton probably never sat under an apple tree. Rather, it is one of numerous simplifications that circulated in the early eighteenth century to popularise his somewhat more extensive observations. There was even an Italian version especially for women: 'Il Newtonianismo per le dame' by a Mr Algarotti, who, together with Voltaire and others, also liked to dine at the court of the Prussian king Frederick II in Sanssouci, announcing the latest ideas of the Enlightenment. And because these are such nice stories, let's leave it at that and not correct anything.

What essentially matters is the fact that suddenly there no longer existed any difference between the laws of heaven and the laws of earth. The old thinking that divided the world into spheres and granted the cosmos an ether that did not correspond to the laws of the earth could no longer be maintained.

But if the forces in heaven and on earth were the same, there was no longer any reason to refer to a divine ether. Newton had literally brought heaven down to earth.

This did not mean, however, that the old world view had to be abandoned. William Whiston was Isaac Newton's successor as professor of mathematics at Cambridge, even appointed by him. Like many of his colleagues, he was a religious follower of 'natural philosophy', whose view of the world was based on the statements of the Bible. Even gravity had been created by the Creator in His infinite wisdom, Whiston and his colleagues were now convinced of this.

Incorporating new knowledge into old beliefs is a phenomenon that is encountered at all times. It's just not always easy to abandon old convictions that had been burned into ones brain for such a long time.

Let there be light

For a society strongly related to the afterlife and the divine heaven, the new thinking had immense consequences. The special nature of heaven suddenly no longer existed. The belief in the 'supernatural' or 'divine' was now questioned. Suddenly, there was no longer a God in heaven watching over earthly events. Nor was there a predetermined destiny to which one had to surrender. Over the next few decades, the world view changed radically.

Religion, however, remained the foundation of a society in which the view prevailed, that the earth was created on 23 October 4004 BC. In 1650, the year of Descartes' death, archbishop James Ussher had precisely calculated the date on the basis of the Bible's chronological data. And God said 'Let there be light! and there was light'. It was a Sunday, of course, at sunrise about eight o'clock in the morning.

His calculations were only a few years away from those of a Johannes Kepler or later an Isaac Newton.

These mathematical calculations also fitted wonderfully into the Christian world view. '*With the Lord, one day is as a thousand years, and a thousand years as one day*', says the Bible (2 Peter 3.8). Almost six thousand years after the creation of the world, many people believed that they were now in the sixth day of the creation story. Some people therefore believed that creation would soon be fulfilled, whatever that might mean. Whiston had calculated the end of the world to be in 1866, Ussher in 1996, while Newton allowed a few more years until the Day of Judgement. It is the perception, that right now humans were at their peak, and that something would be fulfilled very soon. An image that we will encounter again and again over the next centuries.

Despite the new thinking, there was no doubt at all about the Bible and its stories. God had created the world back then on Sunday morning at eight o'clock. Then the Deluge came and destroyed all life. Moses survived, and only afterwards did all civilisation come into being. That's how it was written, that's how it was taught, and that's how it had to be. People adapted their world view to the new circumstances and everything made sense again. That, too, is a phenomenon that will continue for the centuries to come.

Even when Yuri Gagarin was floating in space on board his Vostok for a full one hundred and eight minutes on 13 April 1961, Khrushchev is said to have asked him whether he had seen God. When Gagarin answered with "Yes". Khrushchev paid him ten thousand dollars and advised him to keep quiet. At a later audience with the Pope, Gagarin answered with "No", again received ten thousand dollars, and also with the order to remain silent. Finally, at a meeting with Kennedy, the US President told him that he was now in a free country, where both believing Christians and atheists could live together without any problems. So Gagarin could now tell the truth without any concern, whether he had seen God or not. Gagarin replied: 'Yes, She is black!' Some questions always hold surprising answers.

With the Enlightenment, a very exciting era begins. The effects of this new way of thinking could be observed in all areas, a thinking of being able to change the circumstances of life and no longer having to accept them as given by God. Whereas epidemics and diseases, to which large parts of the population regularly fell victim, had previously been regarded as a god-given event, people slowly began to ask about the causes their causes. So let's now take a look at what the hygienic conditions and medical progress were all about. Let's embark on a journey into regions you would not know before. Let's start in London...

Royal droppings

In September 1665, some fifteen years after Descartes' death, the last great plague epidemic broke out in London and claimed the lives of about one hundred thousand people, about a third of the city's population. In fact, until then, people had no idea of how the disease was transmitted.

The majority of the population still believed in a divine judgement, and attempted to control the situation with prayers and masses. Others believed that bad air was responsible for the disease, and so small fires were now blazing everywhere, in which tobacco, incense or other fragrant substances were burnt. Sometimes even the one or the other pussycat ended up in the flames, because it was also to blame for the plague, they thought. Basically, however, the citizens had no other choice but to close the gates of London, barricade the doors of their houses and wait until the plague had gone away.

The English King Charles II, who had been reinstated in England after the Revolution, fled London with his family and took up residence in Oxford with the entire court. After the plague, when a large part of London was also burnt down in a massive blaze, it seemed to be safe to return home again.

The cleaning staff, who were now moving in, had the very dubious pleasure of putting the Oxford lodgings back in shape. What they found, it is reported, is human faeces in all places of the house. Not only in the cellar they found his royal remains, but behind every curtain and in every corner of every room, whether it was a living room, bedroom, or the kitchen. Even the fireplaces were used as latrines to relieve oneself. His Serene Highness had literally left behind a huge pile of shit.

Until well into the seventeenth century, people had no idea of hygiene or clean sanitary conditions, and these were not exactly at their best. Toilets were rare, and sewage systems were still far from being thought of. For the rural population, none of this was a problem. They could do their business on the nearby dung heap, on a thunderbox, or directly in the field. A good fertiliser it always was.

In the cities, however, the situation was a bid more difficult. Food scraps collected on the streets, mixed with animal cadavers, slaughterhouse waste and the excrement of the city dwellers. Those who could afford it wore high-heeled shoes, so as not to sink ankle-deep into their fellow citizens' droppings.

It is assumed that about one third of the medieval city population died prematurely because of the miserable sanitary conditions. Cities could usually only survive because there was a constant influx of new inhabitants from the countryside to replace those who died prematurely. Living in a city became a cause of death, one might argue.

The sanitary conditions remained to be disastrous. In the completely overcrowded Edinburgh of the eighteenth century, the bells rang at ten o'clock in the evening to signal, that the contents of the faeces buckets could now be disposed of through the window. If a pair of lovers were still in the street at that time, the lady liked to keep close to the house wall to seek shelter from falling evidence of final digestion. After such an unexpected experience, the charmingly fragrant companion was better left outside the door. Even today the gentleman accompanies the lady to the side of the street on the pavement, although he might be unaware where this gallantry stems from.

Very slowly people did begin to understand the connection between hygienic conditions and the outbreak of epidemics. In London, the Royal Society was founded, which Isaac Newton was to preside over for almost twenty-five years. In Paris, the Académie de Sciences was formed, and in Berlin the Royal Prussian Academy of Science. It was not until 1739 that Vienna became the first city in Europe to be completely canalised, long before the first water toilet could finally be installed in the nineteenth century.

From 1710 onwards, efforts were made in England to empirically investigate the causes of the smallpox epidemic. The writer Mary Wortley Montagu, who lived in Istanbul, copied the first 'vaccinations' against smallpox over there and brought this idea to England, and soon the first widespread vaccinations against the disease were carried out. Very gradually, a public health system took hold. Children survived the first years of their lives reasonably unscathed, contributing to the immense population growth that now began. For the first time, people had a real perspective on life.

I stink therefore I am

At the medical faculty of the University of Paris, as everywhere else, teaching was still based on the old method, and that meant sticking to the book knowledge of the last centuries. Medical students were taught the old tale of the four humours, yellow bile, black bile, blood and phlegm, which were to be brought into harmony with each other, and whose imbalance could cause all kinds of illnesses and personal mood swings. That was how it had been learned, that was how it was written, that was how it had to be.

The most terrible martyrdom was probably in wait for you if you fell into the hands of the best doctors at the Sorbonne in Paris. Louis XIV had probably been suffering from excruciating toothache and purulent inflammation of the mouth for some time. So in 1685, at the age of forty-seven, the king had to undergo a problematic extraction of several teeth in his upper jaw. In the process, he not only lost most of his teeth, but also parts of his upper jaw. Of course, the operation was performed without anaesthesia. The king was perhaps even lucky, because sometimes the affected teeth were treated with urine-stained sage, dog excrement or frog fat.

Even worse, however, was the mania for enemas that began with Louis XIV and swept across Europe. The king's personal physician was therefore less concerned about the condition of his majesty's disfigured jaw. After all, he had carefully cauterized the open wound fourteen times with a hot iron. Much more attention was paid to the royal bowels. Regular defecation was a prerequisite for good health, so they had been taught at the Sorbonne. 'Mens sana in colon purifico', his doctor must have thought at the time, 'a healthy mind in a cleansed rectum'.

Since only an empty colon was a good colon, he instructed the supreme ruler of Europe to take a daily elixir of snake powder, incense and horse dung, which proved to be a resounding success, and as the king's health was of public interest, the enema was performed in the presence of the entire court.

It is known from the records of his personal physicians, that Louis had to have his rectum publicly flushed about two thousand times on the advice of his doctors, in order to curb his appetite, which probably stemmed from a tapeworm from which the royal intestines suffered. In one of these years alone he received two hundred and fifteen medicines, especially laxatives, two hundred and twelve enemas and forty-seven phlebotomies.

As a result, the royal terminal digestion had by now acquired the habit of enjoying the utmost health, emptying itself several times a day. It was therefore not unusual for his most exalted excellency to take a seat on a specially prepared throne with a correspondingly circular opening for the royally bare bottom, and to hold his audience in public, accompanied by all the imaginable bodily noises of a illustrious digestive tract tormented by laxatives and enemas. And when the Sun King was perched majestically and loudly proclaimed his state of health, his audience was happy and emulated him.

It was not only at the court in Versailles that enemas now became all the rage. The smelly practice was also copied in other noble houses of Europe, and continued to be used in bourgeois society well into the nineteenth century as a proven means of health care and maintaining a youthful appearance.

The majestic stench that escaped his Serene Highness from every conceivable upper and lower orifice of his body must have been beastly. Even his royal mistress increasingly kept her distance. No wonder, then, that the royal rectum was now bulging out of blinding health, revealing some unsightly ulcers.

Of course, these had to be surgically removed immediately the year after the tooth extraction, but not without having tried out this royal rectal procedure on some 'involuntary volunteers' beforehand. And so His Majesty's personal physician practised on those involuntary volunteers in the hospital at Versailles, some of whom subsequently found themselves in the cemetery.

Fortunately, good doctors were expensive, and so the majority of the population was spared such ordeals. Moliere, the most famous comedy writer of the time, who toured France with his troupe of actors, was not the only one who made fun of this bad habit. His 'Imaginary Invalid' complained, that he had only received eight concoctions and twelve enemas this month, when last month he had received twelve concoctions and twenty enemas. '*It's no wonder that I feel less well this month than the last*', Moliere makes his Argan say. Of course, Moliere played this character himself during the performances.

It remains to mention that he died on stage as the imaginary invalid during the fourth performance of the play, completely without enema.

It was almost a miracle that Louis XIV survived the whole torture at all. Just one month after the operation, the still badly battered royal buttocks were pressed onto a hard church pew in order to hold a thanksgiving mass for the recovery of His Smelling Serene Highness. And so His Majesty the King had to endure the poem 'Le siècle de Louis le Grand', which its author Charles Perrault now recited, praising the superiority of modernity over the long-believed exemplary nature of antiquity. And antiquity at that time meant only Rome.

Since the Renaissance, people have tried to emulate and copy antiquity, not only in medicine, but in all areas, from architecture and literature to philosophy and painting. Antiquity, that is Ancient Rome, was the model to be imitated. And now a Mr Perrault stood before the grandees of society and spoke of France being more progressive than any other culture before. The fact that this sparked off a Europe-wide debate, which is now written up in the history books as the 'Querelle des Anciens et des Modernes' - the dispute between antiquity and modernity - was characteristic of the time of Louis XIV. The king himself was not very interested in this debate, for far more worldly problems plagued him and his royal rear.

Nevertheless, this day claimed one victim. Jean-Baptiste Lully, His Majesty's royal 'surintendant de la musique', with an extraordinary fondness for timpani and trumpets, had performed a specially composed 'Te Deum' for the festivities with one hundred and fifty singers and full orchestral accompaniment.

During the performance, Lully rammed his man sized baton, with which he loudly set the rhythm, onto his own foot with such energy, that he crushed one of his toes. Actually, the toe should now have been amputated, but in view of his king's experience, Lully refused any medical treatment. The wound then became infected with gangrene, and a few weeks later the royal court composer died. Death by baton is therefore a rather rare form of death.

The real breakthrough in medicine did not come until the second half of the eighteenth century. The centre of development was, of course, Paris, the cultural, scientific and political hotspot of Europe at the time, where the ideas of Enlightenment seemed to have progressed furthest.

In pre-revolutionary Paris, the young Antoine Laurent de Lavoisier, the father of modern chemistry, had made new far-reaching discoveries. He developed new instruments and measuring methods, and the results of his experiments contradicted the common conception of the elements. Among others, Lavoisier was able to show, that water is a chemical compound of hydrogen and oxygen, which meant that the four-element theory still taught at universities could no longer be reconciled.

In 1778, the Société Royale de Médecine was founded, of which Lavoisier was also a member. The old curricula of the medical faculty of the Paris University were completely revised. Now it was no longer necessary to study ancient writings within three years, if possible also in Greek and Latin. From now on, observation, practical training, research and science were on the curriculum of medical students.

Paris University now developed into the most modern medical faculty in Europe, attracting scientists and students from all over the world. Hospitals such as the Paris Charité and the Hotel Dieu became a place for research and the treatment of the sick, instead of being used primarily as a gathering place for the sick with a potentially lethal outcome.

With the French Revolution of 1789 at the latest, the new thinking of the Enlightenment had also taken hold in medicine. However, it would take another hundred years before a Louis Pasteur, a Robert Koch and the realisation that diseases are transmitted via different pathogens.

Bouillon rectal

But how long it could take for scientific progress in medicine to fully take hold can be illustrated by another prominent example. In July 1881, the recently elected President of the United States was shot in the back. President Garfield survived the assassination attempt and was actually already on the road to recovery. His martyrdom began, however, when the best doctors in America laid hands on him and tried to remove the bullet from his back.

Against all better judgement, they handled his wounds with unwashed hands and unsterilised surgical instruments, which inevitably led to infections, fever and bed-riddenness. Only the bullet had not been brought out, which is why the latest metal sensors were now being used to locate it. The only thing they forgot was that the springs of his bed were also made of metal, rendering the recordings useless.

Finally, they came up with the idea of simply turning the president on his back and waiting until the bullet fell out on its own, following gravity, so to say, which of course was complete nonsense. But at least it were the best doctors in America who did everything possible for their newly elected president.

For some reason, which is no longer understandable, the crème de la crème of the American medical profession decided to feed their president exclusively through the rectum. So for weeks they poured his 'Bouillon aux boulettes de foie' and a shot of good American whiskey to rinse him into the presidential colon through his buttocks. That the president lost fifty kilos of weight over the next few weeks was acknowledged, but not associated with the unusual dietary method.

When James Abram Garfield finally died of starvation almost three months after the attempted assassination, it must have been a salvation for him.

Very well, after this little excursion into the darkness, let us return to the light of knowledge and fresh air. After so many unwanted glimpses into regions one would not want to see, we'd better quickly change the subject. It is time for a little bit of recuperation.

I suggest a nice mountain lake in the French Alps. So off we go into the clear air to Annecy. Let's see what awaits us there.

Lac du Annecy

Let us enjoy the fresh air and the first warm rays of sunshine of the year in the idyllic panorama of the French Alps. Let's sit down in a nice bistro, have a little aperitif and take time to digest what we already got. There is a Descartes with his mind and a reasonable doubt, and a Newton who brought heaven to earth. At the same time, we have the brutalities of a thirty-year religious war and a revolution in England that was equally violent and religious.

Thomas Hobbes, in his 'Leviathan', which he published shortly after the English Civil War in 1651, said that man is by nature evil, a 'homo homini lupus', that 'man is a wolf to man'. Without the rule of a supreme power, a sovereign, people would be in a state called war, '*where every man is Enemy to every man*'. In such a situation there is constant fear and danger of dying a violent death, '*the life of man, solitary, poor, nasty, brutish, and short*'. It is a view that also justified absolute rule by the French king, who ensured order, security, and above all, a longer life.

The Enlightenment was initially not about shaking up the existing authorities or sovereigns at all. The ideas of the Enlightenment were not even designed for that purpose. On the other hand, if Newton claimed that the rules in heaven were the same as on earth, then the appointment of a king 'by the grace of God' became obsolete. Moreover, were all men really bad by nature, as Hobbes believed? Please enjoy the beautiful nature, the tranquillity and the warming March sun for a little while longer. Because in a moment, a young man will come around the corner who will throw this whole beautiful idyll into great turmoil. À la vôtre - on your health!

It was one of those first sunny days towards the end of March 1728, when the clear midday sun made the last remnants of a cold winter melt away and be forgotten. Here in Annecy, where Mme de Waren had lived since she had fled from her husband some years before, spring was finally beginning. A cold breeze still flowed down from the mountains across the lake at night, but during the day the temperatures were already very pleasant.

Françoise-Louise de Warens was about to celebrate her twenty-ninth birthday and was in the midst of her preparations. At first, she was not at all comfortable with the news, that a young guest, barely sixteen years old, would be arriving this afternoon. She preferred to stay alone, which did not mean that she would have to be without good friends or the fun of a lover or two. Nevertheless, she received an annual pension from the Duke of Savoy with the condition that she should take care of just this kind of young man who was now standing at her door. She had not been told much about him.

His mother had died early, his father had fled, and now the little boy needed a home and a little attention. Mme de Warens knew at first sight that it was not going to be an easy task.

In front of her stood a sixteen-year-old, hormone-controlled youngster in the full bloom of puberty, who couldn't stop staring at her bosom. Normal conversation seemed to be impossible for now, that much was certain. Hoping that the boy's state of mind would soon calm down, she allowed him in and avoided in any way giving him any reason to continue staring at her boobs for the next few days. Her efforts, however, were in vain.

After the first love letter from her new guest had been slipped under her door, and the boy's hormones were still not only shooting into his head and clouding his brain at the sight of her, Mme de Waren decided on the only proper thing to do. She gave him a little hand money, found him a travelling companionship, and sent him to Italy to cool his heels.

And so the young Jean-Jaques Rousseau, as he was named, gained his first sexual experiences in early eighteenth-century Turin, eventually became her lover a few years later, after returning to his 'maman', Mme de Waren, and spent five happy years together with her, or at times in a 'ménage à trois' with one of her other lovers. On one or two occasions he also enjoyed an amorous adventure with preferably mature and charming ladies, which he would never remember without delight, as he later wrote in his biography, the 'Confessions'.

Until then, Rousseau had no sound school education nor had he learned anything properly. There was nothing to suggest that he would ever become the absolute superstar of philosophy. Nevertheless, he turned out to be the 'enfant terrible' in eighteenth-century Paris, challenged the usual social conventions of his time, and with his 'Contract Social' and his views on the education of children, 'Emile', he got into so much trouble with the ruling authorities that he eventually had to flee France.

Rousseau did not see society as inherently at war, as Hobbes believed. For him, man is free by nature, and no one would automatically possess the right of an absolute rule.

> '*Man is born free, and he is everywhere in chains. Those who think themselves the masters of others are indeed greater slaves than they*'.

Rousseau wrote in his 'Social Contract' in 1762. For him, a legitimate rule resulted only from a voluntary agreement among the citizens of a state, for no man by nature exercises authority over another. Power does not produce any kind of justice, Rousseau believed. He believed that there is a common, moral interest for all citizens to organise themselves freely.

> '*To renounce freedom is to renounce one's humanity, one's rights as a man and equally one's duties*', he wrote.

At the height of absolutism in France, Rousseau turned against Louis XV's common conception of the state. In his 'Contract Social', Rousseau opposed the absolute claim of the French king's 'l'etat c'est moi' - the state is me, with the 'volonté général - the overall interest of the community. In this way, he not only spoke out against the king and his absolute rule, but also took up a front against the entire social system of his time.

Rousseau's radical thoughts on human freedom turned all previous ideas upside down. With his ideas of a self-determining community, there was no more reason to have to accept different rights and privileges for the 'citoyens', the citizens of a state. The same rules should and had to apply to kings and princes as to the entire population.

Personal freedom, equality before the law and the 'volonté général' also meant democratic conditions, and it is not for nothing that the French motto later became 'Liberté, Egalité, Fraternité'. Such a democratic society with a self-determining population seemed to be the only logical consequence. The top-down, authoritarian and God-given absolutism of the French kings was suddenly no longer the only conceivable system.

Rousseau is still today regarded as one of the pioneers of modern democracy and of a state in which the citizens themselves should determine their own laws. After his death, he was honoured as a symbol of the French Revolution. In October 1794, the French National Convention had Rousseau's mortal remains transferred triumphantly to the Pantheon in Paris. What seems perfectly normal and natural to us today was an affront to the natural order at the time, a tremendous demand that was not to remain without political consequences.

Actually, people were now facing a huge dilemma. The first thoughts of the Enlightenment were not at all intended to challenge the previous conceptions of a state with a king appointed by God at its head.

But now they reached the point where the ideas of liberty and equality that Rousseau had brought into play no longer fit into the old system. And once the ideas were out in the world, the French Revolution was only a matter of time.

Let's go to Paris, then, and see what happens. But don't worry, we're not going to the barricades now. Instead, we should sit down in one of these new restaurants that have just opened here and enjoy some of the culinary delights that only the French Revolution made possible for us. Take a seat and listen to the story of how it all came about.

The story of haute cuisine

A revolution at times brings about some very strange consequences. Thus, a certain Tobias Schmidt, written with 'dt', had completely unintentionally contributed to the spread of those culinary delights that are still referred to today as the French 'haute cousine'.

Tobias really had nothing to do with cooking. He was actually a piano maker and born in Hesse, and moved to Paris a few years before the revolution hoping to do better business there. However, the demand for pianos in the now revolutionary Paris left much to be desired, as his clientele slowly became scarce. Therefore, he considered himself more than happy to be able to pursue his other passion as an 'inventor of useful instruments', as he later put it himself.

In March 1792, a distinguished physician from Paris stood all of a sudden at his door and asked for his help. 'Good afternoon', said this man, 'my name is Josef Ignazius Guillotin, and the Revolution needs your help'. Doctor Guillotin was once a member of the National Constitutional Assembly and advocated a 'humanization' of the death penalty, because up to now, depending on their crime and their social background, the offenders were being wheeled, quartered, hanged, or massacred in some other cruel way. In the spirit of the French Revolution, this was to be stopped, and 'égalité' and 'humanité' were have to be applied to massacring as well.

When the doctor appeared on his doorstep, Tobias Schmidt with "dt" decided to help the revolution in his very own way. Within a few weeks, the two men developed an apparatus commonly known as the 'rasoir national', better known today as the 'guillotine'.

Beheading now became much faster, much more efficient, and much more humane, they were convinced. And most importantly, it did not discriminate according to the origin or social status of the neck from which the head was to be separated, nor according to the nature of the crime. All people were equal, especially their necks. And this was exactly what was needed in Paris at a time, when prisons were filled with the often rich nobles and clerics who were ordered to be executed.

This, of course, resulted in some side effects that were certainly unintended. As many high-ranking personalities of the 'Old Regime' found themselves increasingly headless on the run or in the cemeteries of Paris, their remaining servants were forced to either find a new profession or a new clientele. Since the food was generally indifferent to the type of stomach it ended up in, many former chefs in revolutionary Paris gradually opened the first really good restaurants where one could dine 'royally', or rather 'princely', provided, of course, that one brought the necessary small money, which was already the case at that time. The first real menus now appeared, which was an enormous progress, unknown in the traditional soup kitchens.

With the French Revolution, the idea of 'égalité', or equality, prevailed in almost all areas. It was not only on the scaffold that everyone was now treated equally, but now pretty much everything was made equal.

Uniform weights and measures were introduced, the different time zones in France were abolished, and for the first time it was the same time for all French people. Also the decimal system, so familiar to us today, was now introduced, so that today one meter is one hundred centimetres.

Only in England, which was otherwise so progressive, there is until today resistance to this system. Around the end of the Seven Years' War and the gradual establishment of a British Empire, the islanders slowly began their special path.

The changeover of the British currency to a decimal system did not take place until 1971, when the country joined the European Economic Community. The day is still celebrated today as 'Decimal Day'. British measures of length, however, are still based on the foot size of some king.

In 2016, older citizens in particular voted to leave the European Union, probably thinking that everything was better in the past. And for them, this 'before' was only about fifty years ago.

Interesting Times

It was not until the French Revolution and the ideas of Rousseau that the idea of democracy and a 'nation state' slowly took hold. The ideas of Descartes and the discovery of Newton 'disenchanted' the world, and challenged the old thinking. Rousseau's idea of a 'social contract', however, now demanded that all people should be equal, all people should be endowed with the same rights, and all people should have the same opportunities to develop. No absolutism in France suited such ideas. When King Louis XVI, alias Citizen Louis Capet, was put under the guillotine, not only his head, but also the whole old system was cut off.

It was the time when something like the idea of a 'nation' started to exist, or rather, in France - the most populous and still most important country in Europe - we now see the beginning of a nation.

On the right bank of the Rhine, the 'Reich', the situation was somewhat different. There, too, the ideas of the Enlightenment were not at all 'national' at first. Some ideas of the Enlightenment had gained acceptance in the ruling houses. Friedrich II of Prussia certainly saw himself as an enlightened monarch, introduced essential reforms, and brought the French philosopher Voltaire to his court right at the beginning of his reign. Nevertheless, this in no way prevented him from launching his endless Silesian Wars against the Habsburg monarchy of Maria Theresa and sending tens of thousands of soldiers to their deaths. 'Old Fritz' was an absolute ruler, and there was no room for a 'volonté général'.

The Habsburg Empress, Maria Theresa, also strongly advocated reforms in her country. Guilds were abolished and the free movement of goods was facilitated. She was open to many innovations, but like 'Old Fritz' in Prussia, she remained arch-conservative by heart, as evidenced by the newly established chastity court, which punished 'indecent behaviour'. Prostitutes were often deported by ship down the Danube to Timisoara and 'settled' there. Even old Giacomo Casanova, that Venetian philanderer who intended to live up to his name in Vienna, had been deported from Vienna because he had been caught 'pissing in the wild'.

When Rousseau published his Social Contract in 1763, the Silesian Wars, or rather the Seven Years' War, had just ended in Europe and worldwide. France had lost its colonies in America to England, and its trading posts in India to the British East India Company. Prussia had annexed Silesia and became a major European power. In England, the situation was a little different. The country was just moving into the economic fast lane. Since George II had been king there, the 'industrial revolution' had gathered pace. As early as 1712, the first steam engine was put into operation in England, setting the 'Industrial Revolution' in motion, and Adam Smith described the first capitalist economic system in his book 'Wealth of Nations' in 1776.

The French Revolution was met with true horror in the ruling houses. A 'Nation' and 'national identity' did not play any role at all in the ruling houses of that time, and it was not even thought of. 'State' and 'Nation' had nothing to do with each other. The ruling families of Europe were mostly closely intertwined, and represented the exact opposite of a 'nation state'.

Maria Theresa had married off her children to all of Europe and now had to watch her daughter Marie Antoinette end up on the scaffold in France. Like his father, the English king came from Hanover, his wife from Celle. In addition to his title as English king, he was also German elector and supreme colonial ruler of the English possessions from America to India.

Most German intellectuals, however, were positively thrilled by the French Revolution. The desire for freedom was now quickly equated with the desire for a state of their own. 'Freedom' and 'nation' became the different sides of the same coin. One needed a 'nation' and the 'nation state' in order to be able to enforce the ideas of the Enlightenment and freedom, so it was thought. No one had foreseen such a development in any way, and no one could guess in which direction Europe would now head.

In the former 'Reich', however, it caused great difficulties for a long time to define 'German' at all. Bohemia, for example, was the heartland of the former 'Reich', but was not supposed to be 'German'. Hanover was 'English', the Habsburg Empire stretched from Austria to Hungary and Croatia. Schleswig was 'Danish', the Alsace 'French'. And then there were the eastern regions of Prussia, which had not previously been part of the 'Reich'. It was an ungodly mess.

When the German 'revolutionaries' in Frankfurts Pauls Chapel agreed on a constitution in 1849, Austria, Bavaria, Prussia, Saxony and Hanover rejected it. Finally, the Prussian king was humbly asked whether he did not intend to accept the imperial crown. Even he must have been somewhat amused by this. In a letter to his sister, the Prussian king called the National Assembly a 'Frankfurt man-donkey-dog-pig-and-cat-deputation' and went on to the order of the day. The revolution is over, the deputies may go home, the last one please turn out the lights. That was all. Revolution and Germans do not go together, it is literally not a German term.

The fact that the call for 'freedom' ended up in Empires first in France and later in the 'Reich' is actually a staircase joke in history. When the Prussian king was appointed emperor in Versailles in 1871, an authoritarian nation state had suddenly been created without the original liberal idea. This is the time when a 'German identity' was created and its founding myths are invented. 'May you live in interesting times', a chiniese curse says, and interesting times these had been indeed.

A bit more peace and tranquility would not be a bad idea, so let the Enlightenment be Enlightenment, hang all these thoughts of revolution and freedom, of 'liberal' and 'national' by the heels and take some time out. Let's leave revolutionary Paris and forget everything that has to do with politics. What we need now is a little sun and a moment of release.

The Adriatic Sea with its beautiful town of Trieste is particularly pleasant in this early summer. Let's go for a short holiday. The Osteria at Trieste's Piazza Grande seems to be a pretty good place to take a time out and relax a little...

Fabricated Stories

Archangel Francesco
Göttingen makes history
An unfinished age
Cocktail Fatal
The story of the German Greeks
Dessert with bad taste

Archangel Francesco

Welcome to Trieste in the old Habsburg Empire. Austria' still reaches to the Mediterranean Sea at this time. If you like, sit down in the Osteria and order something nice for yourself. We are about to meet a man who had next to nothing to do with all the talk of revolution and politics. He wasn't the only one who was getting bored and unintered in all these talks and speeches from so-called experts and intellectuals in their salons. Real life - at least so far - had little or nothing to do with it. However, the person we are about to meet is a very important one, although you have probably heard very little about him up to now. He is above all a fantasist, a dreamer and a aesthete, but not for much longer, as his life will come to a sudden stop very soon. So let's finally start with the story.

It was early June 1768, and at the time this man was travelling incognito through the Habsburg Empire from Vienna to Trieste. He wanted to get back to Rome as soon as possible, was waiting for a ship passage and spent most of the time in the Osteria Grande in the large square in the centre of Trieste, where he had rented a room.

He had no idea that he was shortly to have a very unpleasant encounter with an 'archangel', which was to end for him in a cruel and fatal way. The court records of this act were considered lost for over two hundred years, and still bear witness today to a crime that shook the world of his 'epoch'. These court records report the following event:

On 21 July 1768, Superintendent Zanardi was still standing in the office of the Prefecture of Police of Trieste with somewhat wobbly knees and a slightly pale expression on his face. He handed over a letter to the Inspector of Criminal Investigation, Johann Veit Piechl von Ehrenlieb, who had been investigating a murder case for the last few weeks. The case was actually clear from the start, because the culprit had been clearly identified and convicted. He had been picked up in the mountains while fleeing north and brought back to Trieste. Ehrenlieb read through the letter, the wording of which was as follows:

> *'I, the undersigned, report to this most gracious Imperial and Royal Criminal Court how I had the public death sentence carried out against the prisoner Francesco Arcangeli. It happened at about ten o'clock in the morning on a high scaffold opposite the Osteria Grande, and in such a way that the executioner broke him on the wheel alive, starting from the top and working downwards. His body was then taken to the place called Maina, and there it was placed on a high wheel, where it was to remain until its decay. Thus it is. I, Giovanni Zanardi, Municipal Barigello'.*

Zanardi had to attend the execution of the delinquent that July morning as a witness, and if there was anything positive to report, then it was that the execution was carried out 'from top to bottom'. In the past, or in particularly bad cases, the execution often was carried out in reverse order, starting with the legs. The executioner then smashed the condemned person lying on the floor with a wheel, first the lower and upper thighs, and slowly worked his way up the arms to the shoulders. Often the victim was then put on another wheel while still alive, and the shattered limbs were pulled through the spokes before death occurred or the executioner finally smashed his head with another blow. By 'starting from the top', one could hope that the executioner broke the victim's neck right at the beginning of the procedure.

A good six weeks ago, on 8 June 1768, the police prefect Zanardi had come to Ehrenlieb and told him of a murder. Both then hurried across the piazza to the Osteria Grande, where the crime was supposed to have taken place. When Ehrenlieb entered hotel room number ten, the scene of the crime, he looked past the other people in front of him to the floor where the victim, covered in blood, was lying on a mattress with an ashen, sunken face. A doctor was tending to the wounds from which blood was oozing incessantly.

The victim was still alive and even conscious. '*The villain from room nine next door,*' gasped the man on the floor. Only with the greatest difficulty and with many pauses did he describe the crime and his murderer in the last seconds of his life that remained.

'*I showed him silver coins and two gold coins. The empress had given them to me at Schönbrunn,*' he said. '*Then suddenly - rope around my neck. I fought back. He pulled the knife, stabbed me, I don't know how many times, and fled...'*

This, or something similar, is how the crime is said to have happened, according to the court documents. The victim's neighbour in the Osteria, the 'archangel' Francesco Archangeli, first tried to strangle the victim with a rope. However, the victim was of considerable stature and knew how to defend himself fiercely. When he had almost freed himself from the rope, Francesco Archangeli pulled a knife from his waistband and stabbed his victim seven times, with five of them being fatal.

Why the murder victim was travelling incognito, why he had met the empress before, and what was up with the two gold coins he had received as gifts from Maria Theresa herself will probably forever remain one of the unsolved mysteries of history. The papers found with him identified the murder victim as '*Johannes Winckelmann, Prefect of the Antiquities of Rome, born in Stendal on 9 December 1717, returning to the Holy City*'. That the Prefect of the Antiquities of Rome was murdered by an 'Archangel Francesco' is utterly grotesque.

Up until now, when one spoke of antiquity in Europe, one meant above all the Roman antiquity. Rome was the eternal city and the centre of ancient art, which was still tangible with its countless statues, with the greatest monuments of antiquity and the numerous paintings. Pompeii and Herculaneum had just been excavated, of which Winckelmann had written extensively, thus becoming one of the fathers of archaeology, although he himself had probably never held a spatula or brush in his hand. Anyone who wanted to see art, to experience art, had to come to Rome, and antiquity had just come back into fashion.

Johann Joachim Winckelmann, however, is the most prominent representative who clearly traced antiquity back to ancient Greece, with wide ranging consequences as we might see. He grew up in the late Baroque times with its cherubic angels and scrolls, and the very fond shellwork of the Rococo. The only things that really interested this fantasist were art and ancient Greece. Goethe later remarked:

'As often as Winckelmann rambled about in what was knowable and worth knowing, guided partly by desire and love, partly by necessity, he always came back sooner or later to antiquity, especially to the Greek, with which he felt so closely related and with which he was to unite so happily in his best days'.

After a few bumpy starts, Winckelmann was fortunate enough to be able to work as a librarian near Dresden, and later he continued to find wealthy patrons and benefactors. He had read just about everything that was known about antiquity at the time. He knew the Greek myths, Homer's Iliad and Herodotus' Histories. He knew Plato's works, Xenophon and Diogenes Laertios. And of course he knew the paintings, pictures, statues and everything that somehow had to do with art. However, he could not yet know anything about the long history of Mesopotamia or Egypt.

When he set off for Rome, the Seven Years' War was just breaking out. Fortunately, the city was safe, and for Winckelmann it seemed to be the best time to go there, and as quickly as possible. But he wasn't really looking for Roman history. For him, it was only a copy of the much older, much clearer Greek art.

Greek statues had to shine in bright white, but not painted colourfully like those in Rome. He found his Greek art in everything he looked at in Rome. The Renaissance had still taken Rome as a model, Winckelmann related everything to the Greeks.

When he published his first short work 'Thoughts on the Imitation of Greek Works in Painting and Sculpture' in 1755, he hit the nerve of the time. Against the cherubic angels of the Baroque he set 'the noble simplicity and quiet grandeur' of a Greek antiquity, as he imagined it very fancifully. His book became the catechism of a new art form and of the perception of history in general.

> '*The good taste which is spreading more and more through the world has begun to form first under the Greek firmament,*' he begins his writing. '*All the inventions of foreign peoples came, as it were, only as the first seed to Greece, and took on a different nature and form in the land which Minerva, it is said, before all lands, because of the temperate seasons she encountered here, assigned to the Greeks for their dwelling, as a land which would produce clever minds.*'

Winckelmann met an audience that embraced this fascination enthusiastically and with willingness. He constructed his own Fantasy Land, in which people wandered around looking beautiful, healthy and if possible completely naked. For naked men, Winckelmann had a very particular weakness.

> '*The young Spartans had to show themselves naked every ten days before the ephors, who imposed a stricter diet on those who began to get fat. Yes, it was one of the laws of Pythagoras to beware of all superfluous appendage to the body*'.

The naked men were beautiful, the young women were also beautiful but were at least still allowed to wear short skirts, and both together were very cautious about 'begetting beautiful children'. He even mentions the volte-face politician Alcibiades, '*who in his youth did not want to learn to blow the flute because it obscured his face*'. That's how beautiful the ancient Greeks were.

Even the dress fashions, in which Louis XV could only spend a little time with his official mistress, Madame de Pompadou, if he had first rummaged through the chicken-basket-like arrangement of his playmate's sweeping hoop skirts, were superfluous pomp for him.

> '*After that, the whole suit of the Greeks was such that it did not do the least constraint to*

the forming nature. The growth of the beautiful form suffered nothing from the various types and parts of our present-day pressing and clinging clothing, especially at the neck, hips and thighs'.

Above all, however, the imitation of the Greeks was now on everyone's lips. Whether Heyne, Humboldt or Hegel, this sentence dug deep into the brains of his time. Indeed, he wrote:

'The only way for us to become great, if it is possible, inimitable, is to imitate the ancients'.

While Carsten Niebuhr was on his expedition to the Orient, Winckelmann wrote his second major work, the 'History of the Art of Antiquity' in 1764. This time his imagination had completely run wild. His world of the Greeks was one in which milk and honey flowed. It was bright, sunny and clear, and of course there were no serious diseases there yet, 'which could destroy so many beauties and spoil the noblest creations'. The ancient Greeks now became superhumans in his eyes:

'Through freedom, like a noble branch from a healthy trunk, rose the thought of the whole people. The Greeks in their best time were thinking beings who had already thought for twenty years and more before we generally

begin to think of ourselves, and who occupy the mind in its greatest fire, supported by the vigour of the body, which with us, until it declines, is ignobly nourished'.

The fact that the Greeks had already thought everything imaginable sounds somehow familiar, right?. All Greeks were also extraordinarily wise. '*A wise man was the most honoured, and this was known in every city, as with us the richest'*, he noted. What followed was a hymn to the Greeks. Arts, worldly wisdom, science and historiography, all came from the Greeks.

> *'Their senses, working through quick and sensitive nerves into a finely woven brain, discovered at once the various qualities of a reproach, and occupied themselves chiefly in contemplating the beautiful in the same'. And it was only because the evil Persians conquered the Ionian west coast that the centre of wisdom shifted to Athens, 'where, after the tyrants had been driven out, a democratic regime was introduced in which the whole people had a share, the spirit of every citizen and the city itself rose above all the Greeks'.*

Voilà! If you wanted to know when the glorified picture of Greek history and philosophy began, here you are.

Eduard Meyer, whom we already know from the 'Sea Peoples Saga', portrayed Winckelmann about a hundred years later as the first man,

> *'who, quite independently and with a scientifically educated eye, contemplated the classical creations of art and was so imbued with the sublimity, the harmony, the living breath of them that this ancient spirit was expressed and, as it were, embodied in him in the grainy, simple language, in the principles of his teaching and in the idea of perfect beauty'.*

Of course, Winckelmann himself could not have known what effects his fantasies would have right up to our own time. He really only wanted to depict the history of art as he understood it. And we will see later why the 'Germans' in particular are so fond of it.

The extent to which the image of antiquity had been burned into people's minds can still be seen today in the art galleries and many classicist buildings of the time. Every student of art and architecture must have had Winckelmann's phrase of 'noble simplicity and quiet grandeur' literally slapped around their ears. In almost every city, the magnificent buildings of that almost hundred-year era can be found, and there is always a reference to Greek antiquity, or rather to what was thought to be it.

A hole epoch began with Winckelmann, and the news about his death shook the whole of Europe. Goethe later wrote:

> *'This tremendous incident did tremendous effect; it was a general wailing and lamentation, and his untimely death sharpened attention to the value of his life.'*
>
> And of its influence he later noted:
>
> *'In all efforts, however, which related to art and antiquity, everyone always had Winckelmann in mind, whose efficiency was recognised with enthusiasm in the fatherland. All the journals agreed on his fame, the better travellers returned instructed and delighted by him, and the new views he gave spread over science and life'.*

It is fascinating to see, however, how quickly Goethe turns from Winckelmann's death to his own digestion:

> *'But in lamenting Winckelmann's departure unboundedly, I did not think that I would soon find myself in the trap of being anxious for my own life. Through an unfortunate diet, I spoiled my digestive powers; the heavy Merseburg beer darkened my brain, the coffee, which gave me a very own dreary mood, especially when drunk with milk after dinner, paralysed my intestines and seemed to completely heat up their functions'.*

Well, heavy events can have devastating effects on one's intestines, and we don't know whether Goethe also had an enema or two. Therefore, we prefer to keep the poor poet at a distance and let him continue to flutter at a certain range.

However, this obsession with Greece was not only evident in art and architecture, but also in literature. When Schiller wrote his poem 'Ode to Joy' in 1785, he was well aware about Greek mythology. And at the latest since Beethoven wrote his 9th Symphony in 1824, the 'Ode to Joy' became known throughout the world:

Joy, beautiful spark of Divinity,
Daughter of Elysium,
We enter, drunk with fire,
Heavenly one, thy sanctuary!
Thy magic binds again
What custom strictly divided;
All people become brothers,
Where thy gentle wing abides.

In order to first understand what it is that one so happily and fervently hums along to when 'Beethoven's Ninth' is played, one should perhaps learn a bid German - well - and know where this Elysium is located where this daughter comes from. And guess what, that question leads us directly to Homer, who would be surprised.

But this time not to the Iliad, but to the Odyssey, the second great work of the old Greek poet. There an old sea-god prophesies to Menelaus: '*The gods will lead you to the end of the world, to the Elysian plain, the realm of the blessed, where Zeus' beloved son Rhadamanthys, the fair-haired one, resides*'. Elysium, then, was the place to which the great heroes beloved by the gods were sent after their death and attained immortality.

And who was this Menelaus again, who was facing such an extraordinarily heroic death? Well, he was a king's son and had to flee Mycenae with his brother Agamemnon at a young age. Eventually they found refuge with King Tyndareos in Sparta, and if you've read carefully before, you already know what's coming next. The wife of Tyndareos was called Leda and some years ago she had a rather extraordinary encounter with a swan, laid two eggs after the frivolous interlude and thus became the mother of quadruplets of two fathers. Helena, Clytemnestra, Castor and Pollux were their children's names.

Helena was now courted by pretty much all the marriageable young and not-so-young heroes of Greece. And so, for the sake of peace, all suitors were sworn to recognise Helena's choice and to protect the future couple. Thus the beautiful Helen chooses Menelaus, whom she already knew from her childhood. Agamemnon, on the other hand, marries her sister Clytemnestra. It comes as it must, for otherwise we would not have such beautiful stories.

Already the ancient Greeks knew, that childhood sweethearts do not last forever, and so, after a few years, Paris drops by Menelaus' house, kidnaps the beautiful Helen, who not seems to come with him entirely unwillingly, and together they set off for Troy. And since all the Greek heroes had previously sworn an oath to protect the couple, the Trojan War began.

Anyway, thank you, Mr. Schiller, for bringing us back to the beginning of the story. But no matter, one encounters Elysium quite innocently even in Paris, for example when strolling along the Champs Élysées or when the French president receives his guests in the Élysée Palace.

However, it is not quite clear whether Schiller's 'gentle wing' really means that of the swan into which Zeus transformed himself to seduce Leda. But that is for others to clarify.

Mr Schiller was of course not the only author who was fascinated by the myths and stories of Ancient Greece. In 1779 Goethe wrote his 'Iphigenia on Tauris', and he too was well versed in Greek literature. Especially with the works of the ancient Greek tragedian Euripides, who, as you know, was mauled by dogs.

Euripides wrote a play called 'Iphigenia in Aulis', which describes how Agamemnon has gathered with his Greeks in Aulis, but cannot sail to Troy until he has sacrificed his eldest daughter Iphigenia to the goddess Artemis. Iphigenia is already on her way to see her father and the Greeks off to Troy with the whole family, suspecting no evil. Her father tries to warn her, but Agamemnon's brother Menelaus, husband of the beautiful Helen and Iphigenia's uncle, prevents this, whereupon she is sacrificed.

You see, Greek dramas have it all. They are not only much older, but also far more interesting and multi-layered than all the other family tragedies you would like to have heard about in the last few hundred years.

In Goethe's case, however, Iphigenia was not sacrificed but taken to Tauris by the goddess Diana, the Roman version of Artemis. Iphigenia meets Orest, her younger brother, who in the meantime had murdered his mother Clytemnestra, since she had previously murdered his father, who had previously sacrificed Iphigenia, and so on and so forth.

In the end, Goethe's story ends well and everyone returns home safely. We will leave it at that and will not return to the story of the swan. What matters is that ancient Greece was on everyone's lips at the time.

Now that you have finally finished eating at the Osteria, we can get back on the road. We have to go to some lectures at the university in Berlin, and on the way there we make a detour to our old familiar university of Göttingen, it's on the way, so to speak.

It was from there that Winckelmann's ideas and conceptions were disseminated. So, all aboard, next stop Göttingen...

Göttingen makes history

Until the time when Winckelmann wrote his views on the history of Greek art, there was no reason at all to scientifically deal with the past. After all, the Bible, in which the history of mankind was clearly recorded, was available. The world came into being on Sunday 23 October 4004 BC, Noah had survived the Deluge, and after that all the civilisations came into being. The ancient history was written down in the Bible, and after Jerusalem, Rome became the navel of the Christian world, and its history was known quite precisely.

Now with Winckelmann came the view that history did not come from Rome, but from Greece, as he had described in his books. This is now where the University of Göttingen comes into play again, a place where many of the different ideas interwove and led to new thoughts. Until then, all universities had been focused on the classical education of theology, medicine and law. Göttingen now formed an absolute exception. After its foundation in 1734, entirely new disciplines were introduced and the professors were allowed to conduct unhindered research without any censorship. Old Professor Michaelis was thus able to send an expedition with Carsten Niebuhr to Arabia.

At that time, it was also normal for people of different nations to live in one state. Nation and state had almost nothing in common. Now, however, the terms gradually began to get intermingled, and nation and state started to be understood as almost identical, which proved to be quite problematic in the 'Reich' with its more than three hundred states and the different nations.

Obviously, interest in a common history flourished, and Göttingen was emerging as a forerunner in this domain. Seemingly everyone of prominence and importance studied there, be it a Freiherr vom Stein, a Knigge, a Gauss, the Humboldt brothers or later the Grimm brothers. Each of them passed through Professor Heyne's class and listened to his lectures on the 'Archaeology of Ancient Art'.

Heyne himself was in close contact with Winckelmann in Rome, made the concept of a coherent history of art the subject of academic teaching, and spread Winckelmann's ideas and views on the Greeks from Göttingen. '*Art was the literature of antiquity*', the professor believed, '*and the highest perfection of art was achieved by the Greeks*'. He thus triggered a wave of enthusiasm among the young students who listened to him.

Thus, from 1772, the young Johann Heinrich Voß listened to his lectures, the young man who later fuelled the Greek euphoria with his translation of the Iliad and other works. In the same year, he founded the 'Göttinger Hainbund', an association of young writers and artists of the 'Sturm und Drang' period, who indulged in the emotional exuberance of nature and Greek antiquity, an attitude that is difficult to comprehend today. It was the time when Goethe published his 'Sorrows of Young Werther', which was condemned by some as 'unchristian' and 'contrary to all decency'. The group formed an antithesis to the more rational Enlightenment that begun with persons like René Descartes over a hundred years ago.

The euphoria for Greece that emanated from Göttingen at the time seemed to have no limits. Wilhelm von Humboldt was just twenty years old when he matriculated at Göttingen University in 1787. He also sat in on Mr Heyne's lectures, as did later a Georg Grotefend, whose friend Fiorillo established the subject of art history at the university in 1799, based of course on the views of a Mr Winckelmann.

'I hear archaeology with Heyne in the large library hall, with Spittler the history of the latest world affairs, with Lichtenberg a private lecture on light, fire and electricity, and with Heyne the Iliad, where there are about fifty listeners... Heyne is indisputably the brightest man and in certain subjects the most educated in Göttingen'.

These lines were written by Alexander von Humboldt, who, like his brother, of course also studied in Göttingen. He and his brother Wilhelm never attended school. Wealthier families had a private tutor, and after they had exhausted their family library, the two brothers moved to nearby Berlin. There, meanwhile, Literary Salons mushroomed, where the latest achievements in science and literature were discussed, and where reports of the latest discoveries were the first to spread. Louis Antoine de Bougainville and Georg Forster had recently circumnavigated the world and published their travel reports. For the two Humboldt brothers, it must have been paradise to read their books, which reported from a completely different world.

Bougainville described the sexual liberality and promiscuity of the Tahitians. '*Love was the only passion of young women there*', he noted, and '*everything invites them to follow the inclination of their heart or the instinct of their sensuality*'. Apparently, even the ship's chaplain succumbed to these sexual temptations. His host Orou, in fact, left him his wife and three daughters, but advised the clergyman to choose the youngest as his bedmate, as she had no children yet.

> *'You have eaten, you are young, you are well; if you sleep alone you will sleep badly; a man needs a companion by his side at night. Here is my wife, here are my daughters: choose the one that suits you; but if you want to do me a favour, you will give preference to the youngest of my daughters, who has no children yet.'*

The poor clergyman is said to have risen several times in terror during the night, exclaiming: '*But my religion? But my status?*' while he was enjoying himself with Thia, the youngest of the three daughters. At least that is what is written in the 'Supplément au Voyage de Bougainville', written by Denis Diderot, a French writer and philosopher who was known all over the place in his time. After this report, Tahiti became the wet dream of the South Sea of all uptight young men of that time.

Later, at the age of 18, Georg Forster sailed around the world with Captain Cook and, like Bougainville, came to Tahiti. Forster's rather scientific travelogue made the young man suddenly famous. Back in London, he published his book 'A Voyage Round The World', initially in English. Together with the universal genius Rudolf Raspe, whom we already know from Baron Münchhausen tall tells, he then produced the German translation. Raspe was simply a 'polymath' whom one meets again and again.

When Forster returned to Göttingen, he married Therese Heyne, the daughter of the famous Göttingen professor. Of course, the young Alexander von Humboldt did not miss the opportunity to take a short trip along the Rhine to London with the circumnavigator. It was an inspiration for his later research trip to America.

Therese Heyne, her friend Caroline Michaelis, daughter of the professor who sent Carsten Niebuhr on his journey to Arabia at the time, and three other famous daughters of high-ranking Göttingen professors were fondly referred to as 'university damsels'.

They were five emancipated, intelligent and highly educated women who unfortunately seemed to live in the wrong time, and who constantly broke with the encrusted conventions of their environment. To detail all the personal connections would certainly go too far here, but these five 'university damsels' formed something of a gravitational centre around which many of the most famous German intellectuals circled like moths, be it Goethe, Schelling, the two Schlegel brothers and the two Humboldts, Lichtenberg, Fichte, Novalis, Forster, and many more. It was a turbulent time, and the French Revolution soon raged around them. It can therefore hardly come as a surprise that this group also shared similar views, such as those on ancient Greece.

For Wilhelm von Humboldt, the Greek spirit was 'an ideal of what we ourselves would like to be and produce'. The 'imitation of the Greeks' became the postulate of their time. Humboldt wrote:

'Their advantages over us are of such a kind that their very unattainability makes it expedient for us to imitate their works, and beneficent to recall to our minds, pressed by our dull and narrow-hearted situation, their free and beautiful ones'.

When Humboldt was later appointed by Baron von Stein to reform the educational system in Prussia - Stein himself had studied in Göttingen, of course - the old three-tier division at the universities, with theology, medicine and law, was abolished.

From this moment on, all the distorted ideas of Greek antiquity were incorporated into the new educational canon and taught at schools and universities. Even when Sigmund Freud travelled to Athens in 1904, he wrote to a friend in full amazement: 'So all this really exists as we learned it at school'.

History itself is the stories that you are told, that you tell yourself, and that you believe to be true. And Göttingen was the first and most famous university to tell a whole new story. It was probably the most important nucleus from which the image of an ancient Greece spread that still shapes our view of history today. The university, and with it above all Professor Heyne, laid the foundation for later historical scholarship. From now on, the knowledge of Greek antiquity was assumed to be a basic condition for any cultural achievement.

'With the Greeks we have before us a nation under whose fortunate hands everything that, according to our innermost feeling, preserves the highest and richest human existence, had already ripened to its final perfection ... Their knowledge is not merely pleasant, useful and necessary, only in them do we find the ideal of what we ourselves would like to be and produce; if every other part of history enriches us with human wisdom and human experience, we draw from the contemplation of the Greeks something more than earthly, indeed almost divine'

It was Wilhelm von Humboldt who wrote down these lines in 1807, and it was him, who founded the Berlin University in 1810, where Hegel later proclaimed his own version of history. Hegel did not belong to the immediate circle of the Göttingen University, but from him we soon receive a history of philosophy and a philosophy of history that is equally strongly influenced by Winckelmann's views. In the meantime, an image of Greece had solidified among most intellectuals that was only fifty years old.

It's about time for us that we finally set out for Berlin. From now on, as you will see, history will be invented. The same applies to Greek philosophy, which is still so fondly recounted today. Where this all can lead to if one misunderstands the stories of a Mr. Winckelmann and a Mr. Hegel will be seen later. But for now, let's go to Berlin, we have to hurry a bit, for Napoleon is already on his way...

An unfinished age

Lets remember Archbishop Ussher and his calculation that creation took place on a Sunday, 4004 BC. It is the concept of the old thinking that everything started for a particular purpose, everything has a particular meaning and everything makes sense. Underlying this concept was also the idea that the world was completed on the sixth day of creation, because on the seventh day the Lord rested. A thousand years is a single day, as the Bible says. Almost six thousand years had already passed, and soon something would be fulfilled according to this idea. No one really could say exactly what it would be. But the idea of an end to history, of a meaning and a purpose to human existence was still widespread.

The story of Sîn-lēqi-unninni was still buried undiscovered under metre-thick layers of earth in the library of Ashurbanipal in Nineveh. Rousseau had written his social contract, the first restaurants were opening in Paris, Napoleon was back from Egypt, and the young Champollion had just been sent to the school of the Abbé Dussert by his big brother, but was already fainting a time or two. When Napoleon finally set out to conquer Europe, the national sentiments of many young intellectuals boiled up. Those who were in favour of the French Revolution today could be bitter opponents of Napoleon tomorrow. For some, Napoleon had betrayed the idea of revolution; for others, he was only now bringing it to them. It was no different for the 'university damsels' from Göttingen and their admirers. It was a wild hustle and bustle, nobody really knew how they had got from Enlightenment to Revolution, and finally to the Emperor.

So, here we are at the University of Berlin, in March 1806, where a then celebrated and very well-known professor was giving some lectures on 'the basic principles of the present era', just a few months before Napoleon was to invade Prussia.

It is also the time when that turgid, overblown philosopher's German language was slowly to emerge which makes one bang one's head on the table. From this time onwards, many translations were produced that gave the impression that the people in antiquity had already spoken in such a pompous manner. The 'old man' from Königsberg, Immanuel Kant, still had the charm of a boring archivist. He was pedantically precise and about as interesting as Aristotle. That's probably why the two got along so well. Kant's works sometimes read like a telephone directory, but without full stops.

With Johann Gottlieb Fichte, so the name of the young professor we now meet, the language slowly becomes a little more pathetic and sublime, like Winckelmann. But it's not until Hegel that you later need a translator and a helmet. But that is just a little forewarning. Now let's listen to the professor for a moment. So what did Fichte say about history. Well, for him, history made sense and was heading towards something. '*The purpose of mankind's life on earth is that in it, it should establish all its relations with freedom according to reason*', Fichte said. The purpose is reason, quite the Enlightenment man, one would think. Kant had also spoken up for Fichte at the time.

What has a purpose, of course, also has a plan, and Fichte's 'world plan' had five different phases. It is a picture that emerged from the calculations of a Mr Ussher, with his creation in six days and so on. The five epochs of the 'world plan' resemble the education of a child, i.e. from kindergarten and primary school to grammar school and university. The fifth and last age, Fichte was convinced, is the one '*when humanity builds itself up with a sure and infallible hand into the perfect imprint of reason: the state of perfect vindicatioin and healing*'. Thus everything has a beginning and an end, is part of a great 'world plan', and has a deeper meaning. In what Fichte sees this is completely irrelevant here. What does matter is that this idea fitted in very well with the idea that a new age was about to come.

Who came the following year, however, was Napoleon, who stood at the gates of Berlin, which absolutely did not fit into Fichte's 'world plan'. Now '*the state of perfect vindication and healing*' should have come, but definitely not a Napoleon with his French troops. The professor was so upset about this that he felt compelled to write a whole series of very patriotic 'addresses to the German nation', for which he is still known today.

Kant had demanded that people use their own mind. Fichte had assumed that the world is rational. Mind and rationality, however, are not always the same. Fichte believed he could recognise certain regularities in history. Once these were recognised, he believed, statements could be made about the future.

It is the concept that everything makes sense, that history has a beginning and an end, that the world began on a Sunday morning at eight o'clock and will soon come to an end, in other words that there is a 'world plan'.

The trouble with great plans is, however, that they usually go horribly wrong. This was not only the case with Fichte's world plan, but also with Malthus's population forecasts. It is impossible to forecast the future, and here lies the crucial point.

If you look at something from the viewpoint of the end, you are already at the end of a development and can therefore look back into the past. Only then one can 'understand' the development quite precisely and suspect a 'plan' behind it. Only then one can assume a 'sense' for everything and assign it to a certain purpose.

However, if you look at a development from the starting point, there is usually more than one alternative available. One can only assume the development. One has to know the starting point in order to be able to evaluate the next step.

In the end, it is again and still the old argument between 'meaning and purpose', and 'cause and effect'. History makes no 'sense'. When there is no 'sense', there is, of course, no 'plan' either. And when there is neither a 'sense', nor a 'plan', then there is certainly no 'purpose' either. There is only 'cause and effect'. It is the old familiar game that we encounter again and again. But let us continue in our story.

Obviously, Fichte was utterly disappointed that his 'world plan' did not work. From being a supporter of the French Revolution, he had rapidly turned into an opponent of Napoleon, and died as a result of the war.

Well, not that he had personally engaged in the fighting, but rather that he had caught 'typhus' from his wife, who had caught the disease while she was working as a nurse in one of the military hospitals. It's just that they weren't medically ready yet.

We can remain seated on the benches, because Fichte's successor is about to arrive, and he has something even better than just a 'world plan'. The auditorium is still being redecorated a bit. We wait a few more years until 1819. In the meantime, Napoleon suffers his Waterloo, the Congress of Vienna is dancing, and the clocks are turned back again. Revolution was slowly becoming a nonissue. A 'German nation' still did not exist.

Cocktail fatal

Ladies and gentlemen, thank you for staying so long. The renovation work has been completed, the altar has been installed and we are about to meet the famous Mr. Hegel. He is about to take you by the hand

and will explain how the world is working. Don't worry, Hegel will be able to do that, even if you will probably need a translator. Perhaps that's why he is becoming so famous in his church. Somehow, he hit the nail on the head.

However, the whole situation was really a delicate mess. The Enlightenment tried to explain the world rationally with 'cause and effect', keeping all the magic, superstition and witchcraft out to create truly certain knowledge. And after years of work it becomes more and more obvious that a nation state was needed to be able to enforce all these great ideas of 'liberté, egalité, fraternité'.

And finally, out of a sudden, one had to face the problem that all that rational thinking will not fit in with all this national sentimentalism that was caused in the course of this development. Whatever way you do it, you do it wrong.

But it cannot last much longer now. Better put your coats on the tables in front of you so that it doesn't hurt so much when you bang your forehead on them. Half the Prussian state apparatus is sitting in the front benches and is already getting excited.

And there he comes, strolling in wearing the black robe of the chief preacher, passing the packed rows of his frantic followers cheering him loudly. Curtain up for Super-Hegel. Now he stretches out his arms and starts addressing his congregation:

> *'History is mind clothing itself with the form of events or the immediate actuality of*

nature. The stages of its development are therefore presented as immediate natural principles. These, because they are natural, are a plurality external to one another, and they are present therefore in such a way that each of them is assigned to one nation in the external form of its geographical and anthropological conditions.'

While some of the audience in the front rows gasp for breath and the one or the other fainting attendee can be observed, the 'poc-poc' of a whole row of heads banging on tables can be heard from the backbenchers. Unimpressed and with great enthusiasm the professor continues:

'The nation to which is ascribed a moment of the Idea in the form of a natural principle is entrusted with giving complete effect to it in the advance of the self-developing self-consciousness of the 'World-Spirit. This nation is dominant in world history during this one epoch, and it is only once that it can make its hour strike. In contrast with this its absolute right of being the vehicle of this present stage in the development of the 'World-Spirit', the spirits of the other nations are without rights, and they, along with those whose hour has struck already, count no longer in world history.'

Frenetic applause from the first rows. Hats were thrown through the air and the Prussian flag was waved. Yeehaw, finally we are back on stage again. First patriotic shouts for the 'Fatherland' are heard. The community is overjoyed and celebrates its superhero. In case you didn't understand a word, you are in for the same fate as so many others. No worries, I told you it was going to get turgid now.

Hegel is a preacher, and that is not by accident. He was a trained theologian. To him, philosophy was worship. After all, one doesn't have to understand sermons, one has to believe them. That is not only the case in the church, but also everywhere where people clap their hands. When people start applauding, it seems, their brains automatically switch off.

However, let's come to what Hegel actually meant. For him, everything has a meaning, and not only that. In fact, everything has a 'higher' meaning, and a final purpose on its top. Hegel had discovered the 'World-Spirit', according to which every nation has its right to exist. By the time it comes to power, it will determine the history of the world. And it can only do so once. So, first it was the turn of the French, now it was finally Prussia's turn.

While Fichte was still getting upset about Napoleon and was going to the barricades, to Hegel even the slaughter on the battlefields had a higher meaning. Although persons like Napoleon followed their own interest, they were at the same time bearer of the 'World-Spirit'. Unconsciously, therefore, he was only implementing the will of this 'World-Spirit':

'Such are all great historical men – whose own particular aims involve those large issues which are the will of the World-Spirit... Such individuals were practical, political men. But at the same time they were thinking men, who had an insight into the requirements of the time – what was ripe for development. World-historical men – the Heroes of an epoch – must, therefore, be recognized as its clear-sighted ones; their deeds, their words are the best of that time. But so mighty a form must trample down many an innocent flower – crush to pieces many an object in its path.'

Oops, the innocent flower. So, when it rips the guts out of soldiers on a battlefield, it is predestination and serves the 'World-Spirit'. But let's continue with his conception of history. Where has reason gone?

Oh, I see, according to Hegel, reason rules the world. And because reason rules the world, world history is also reasonable. And when world history is reasonable, then there are no coincidences. And when there are no coincidences, then everything is 'divine providence'. Hegel makes it sound like this:

'Divine Providence is Wisdom, endowed with an infinite Power, which realizes its aim, viz., the absolute rational design of the World. Reason is Thought conditioning itself with perfect freedom. (...) History is the exhibition

of the divine, absolute development of Spirit in its highest forms – that gradation by which it attains its truth and consciousness of itself.

So by now Hegel has connected the Enlightenment and the religious ideas of his time, and on top of that also explained why Napoleon was in Berlin. The only question that remains is what he is doing with regard to freedom. Of course, Hegel has an answer to that too, and ends his prayers as follows.

> '*Germany was swept by the victorious French armies, but German nationality shook off this pressure. The lie of an empire has completely disappeared. It fell apart into sovereign states. The principles of freedom of property and of the person have been made fundamental principles. Every citizen has access to state offices, but skill and usefulness are necessary conditions.*
> *Government rests in the civil service, and the personal decision of the monarch is at the head, for a final decision is absolutely necessary. But with fixed laws and a certain organisation of the state, what has been left to the sole decision of the monarch is to be regarded as little in view of the substantial. However, it is to be considered a great happiness when a noble monarch is assigned to a people.*

If you now jump up and briskly beat your boots together, you have done everything right. The front ranks were all aflutter. Being a civil servant - that was even better than the French Revolution! And he, the king, calls the shots.

With Hegel, one can get the impression that he takes all the ideas and conceptions he finds, the entire Enlightenment, the mind, the reason, the religion, the romanticism, the nation, the freedom, the rationality, the feelings, and everything else, that he puts them into a party mixer, shakes them vigorously, and out comes the 'World-Spirit' and the Prussian king.

That is exactly what was needed in the post-Napoleonic era. Not any revolutionaries, but loyal civil servants. There was no more a need for a plan as Fichte thought. Hegel had encountered the 'World-Spirit' that regulates everything and provides a higher meaning for everything.

In fact, we are no longer in the Enlightenment era, but already in the midst of the exuberant emotional world of 'German idealism', in the midst of 'noble simplicity and quiet grandeur', combined with the religious imagination of his time. Hegel is not looking for 'causes and effects', he is looking for the 'meaning and purpose' of world history. One had just been going round in circles for the last two hundred years since Descartes, one would think. One is inevitably reminded of Goethe's Doctor Faust: *Now here I am, a fool for sure, no wiser than I was before!*

However, take a deep breath and please remain seated, as the next lecturer is already waiting for you.

Because, if the history of the world has a higher meaning, as Hegel said, then so does the history of philosophy, of course. This is pure logic, and Super--Hegel is about to explain now, why 'the Germans' are so absolutely fond of the ancient Greek philosophers. I hope you still remember, and the explanation is coming now. So here we go...

The story of the German Greeks

So, what do the 'Germans' have in common with the ancient Greeks? By now we are already familiar with Hegel's sermons on the 'World-Spirit' and can dispense with long introductions. Curtain up, Hegel enters the pulpit, stretches out his arms again and begins his preachment this time as follows:

> *'We shall see in the History of Philosophy that in other European countries in which the sciences and the cultivation of the understanding have been prosecuted with zeal and with respect, Philosophy, excepting in name, has sunk even from memory, and that it is in the German nation that it has been retained as a peculiar possession. We have received the higher call of Nature to be the conservers of this holy flame'.*

The 'Germans' are going to make it great again, I tell you. The 'German nation' will become the torch-bearer of philosophy and the executor of the 'world spirit'. What a wonderful prospect. The banners were rolled out again, and once more shouts of 'fatherland' echoed through the first rows of the audience.

> *'The name of Greece strikes home to the hearts of men of education in Europe, and more particularly is this so with us Germans. The here, the present, art and science, that which in giving liberty to our spiritual life, gives it dignity as it likewise bestows upon it ornament, we know to have proceeded from Greece.'*

Voila! There we have the answer to our question why the 'Germans' are so fond of the Greeks. It took a little while, I know, but perhaps it was worth waiting for. Mr. Winckelmann would certainly be very pleased with these words, and indeed Hegel now begins with a long encomium on the Greeks, because the Germans and the Greeks actually have so much in common: the sense of home, the people, the contentedness, the sociability, actually the Germans are nothing but ancient Greeks, one might think.

> *'The spirit, immersed in nature, is in substantial unity with it (...), the richness of the Greek world consists only in an infinite amount of beautiful, lovely, graceful details, in this serenity in all existence. The greatest thing among the Greeks are the individualit-*

ies: these virtuosos of art, poetry, song, science, righteousness, virtue.'

So preached Hegel, and that was exactly what many people in his time thought. After Napoleon, the age of Biedermeier was just beginning in Germany. People were fed up with revolutions. They retreated into privacy, enjoyed the 'German Gemütlichkeit' (German cosiness) at coffee parties, and cultivated their love of their homeland and of the countryside. Everything was in perfect order, and people did all the things they had in common with the ancient Greeks. It was a contemplative time when you walked through the city like that:

Look, there walks Mr. Biedermeier, and his wife, his son on her arm; his tread is as gentle as on eggs, his motto: Neither cold nor warm.

For the sake of the utmost idyll, the centre of the German philhellenes had soon shifted to Bavaria (Baiern). Here, the Bavarian 'Gemütlichkeit' now sat hand in hand with the Greek antiquity on the mountain hut and looked up at the blue-white Bavarian sky.

Out of sheer emotion, the royal Bavarian decision was made in 1825 to write the name of Baiern with a Greek 'y' (Bayern). A little later, when the now Bavar(y)an prince also became King of Greece, the new Greek national flag had to be blue-white of course, as like the Bavar(y)an. History sometimes takes remarkably bizarre paths.

Of course, now the question arises as to what was before and after the Greeks. And of course Hegel had an answer. The 'Oriental' preceded the Greeks and, of course, but had no philosophy. The 'Oriental' only possessed a religion that came close to philosophy. The 'Oriental' was simply not that far civilized yet, nor was 'the Chinese' or 'the Indian'. Also "the Romans" and "the Teutons" did not come off too well with Hegel. The Jurisprudence came from the Romans, and the Teutons first had to be bonded by the church to learn to appreciate their freedom. But now came 'the German', who had gone through all that. Now it was their turn. They were Prussian officials, a torch-bearer of philosophy, and the king decided which way to go. How beautiful!

Finally, Hegel bluntly brings religion back into play, in the hope,

> *'that in addition to the kingdom of the world (...) the Kingdom of God may also be considered. In other words, along with the business of politics and the other interests of every-day life, we may trust that Science, the free rational world of mind, may again flourish'.*

Hegel was and remained a full-blooded theologian. Reason and religion were almost identical to him. Two hundred years after Descartes and Newton, a very large circle closes with Hegel, and suddenly we are back at the very beginning of history. Faith and religion are now 'pure science' and the 'free rational world of the spirit'. Hegel's 'World-Spirit' was nothing but a God who predestined everything.

For a 'real enlightener', the stomach just turns. Instead of 'cause and effect' we now have 'meaning and purpose' again. Perhaps Kant should have given his colleagues a good kick up the backside to get them to switch on their mind again.

Mind and reason are really not congruent. What was science with Kant became religion with Hegel. When Kant died in 1805, the great age of enlightenment in 'Germany' was over, and apparently the mind also ceased to exist.

For Hegel, the history of philosophy is the 'World Spirit', which, like a giant computer, has been working secretly on the programme 'Reason' for two and a half thousand years, and the result was 'religion'.

> '*Tantae molis erat, se ipsam cognoscere mentem - All this time was required to produce the philosophy of our day; so tardily and slowly did the World-Spirit work to reach this goal*', Hegel ends his lecture.

Another computer, the hyper-intelligent pandimensional supercomputer 'Deep Thougt', came up with the result '42', although the question had been asked incorrectly right in the beginning. Before the computer was even switched on, it started with Descartes' 'I think therefore I am' and had already discovered the existence of rice pudding before it could be switched off again, at least if you trust Douglas Adams' 'Hitchhiker's Guide to the Galaxy'.

In contrast to Descartes in Ulm, the author in Austria had given himself over to beer at a German Oktoberfest when the idea for his cult novel came to him in a drunken stupor. So it works with alcohol, too, and 'The Hitchhiker's Guide' is certainly more fun than Hegel's lectures. Fantasy novels and philosophy have a lot more in common than one might think. That was already the case with the ancient Greeks.

All these weird fantasies started with Winckelmann. Via Göttingen, Heyne, Goethe, Schiller, Humboldt and many others, they finally reached Hegel, and even today many are firmly convinced that it all began with the Greeks. The only way to debunk this whole hoax is probably to remember Descartes and ask a very simple question: Why the Greeks?

If no one can answer this question, it is probably because the question has been asked wrongly. Nothing started with the Greeks, and there was never a computer programme running in the background. It's just a really good story that people may or may not believe. Or, to put it in the words of Friedrich Nietzsche:

> *'Winckelmann's and Goethe's Greeks, Victor Hugo's Orientals, Wagner's Edda personages, Walter Scott's thirteenth-century Englishmen - at some point you will discover the whole comedy! it was All beyond measure historically wrong, but – modern'.*

Dessert with bad taste

We will now take a look at what can become of a story that goes completely off the rails. We have to anticipate some things that will only be worked out in later chapters. But it is worth making this little excursion into the future.

Hegel died in Berlin in 1831 and was one of the most famous philosophers of his epoch, not only in a 'Germany', which still did not exist. After 'the Germans' had been busy almost exclusively with themselves and their 'nation', the 'German Empire' finally was proclaimed in 1871 in national exuberance. The idealised image of ancient Greece survived this period unscathed and grew even stronger.

In the meantime, many had become convinced of the superiority of the 'white race' or, better, of the 'Caucasian type'. We will see later where these thoughts came from. This idea of the superiority of the white man fell on fertile ground especially in America and England. Even today, when entering the USA, people are still asked about their 'race'. Chambers book form 1844 'Traces of the Natural History of Creation' became a real bestseller of the time, and it makes the following statement:

> *'The human race is known to consist of numerous nations, offering considerable differences in outward form and colour, and generally speaking different languages. The leading characters of the different races of man-*

kind are, in short, simply representations of the different stages of the development of the highest or Caucasian type

In France, Joseph Arthur de Gobineau made a name for himself when he emphasised the alleged superiority of the Aryan in terms of intelligence and energy in his 1853 book 'Attempt on the Inequality of the Human Races'.

A few years later, Francis Galton, actually a respected geologist, felt called to improve the 'white race' and saw considerable differences in the mental capacity. In doing so, he warned against the spread of the black population, especially in the USA. '

There are now some 8 million of Negroes in lands where not one of them existed twelve generations ago, and probably not one representative of the race which they displaced remains there,' he warns in his 1859 book 'Heredity Genius', thus becoming the founder of eugenics.

The irony of the matter was that Galton was a cousin of Charles Darwin, who had just published his book 'On the Origin of Species' a few years earlier. Only Galton had completely misunderstood his cousin.

Men were just racing full steam ahead into the racist delusions of the nineteenth and twentieth centuries. However, they were not the slightest bit aware of this, as they were utterly convinced that they could derive all of it scientifically.

Against this background, an image of Greece was developed in Germany, in which the Greeks were described as the 'most gifted of all peoples'. After all, the Germans were also the 'torchbearers of Greek philosophy' and soon were to become the executors of the 'world spirit'.

It was the time in which the Ionian natural philosophers were 'invented', the first rationally thinking scientists in world history, and the 'Germans' were in direct line with them. From Eduard Zeller comes something like the following from 1876:

> *'Only the Greeks acquired that freedom of thought that they did not turn to religious traditions but to the things themselves in order to learn the truth about the nature of things; only with them did a strictly scientific procedure, a cognition that follows only its own laws, become possible'.*

The ideas about the Greeks were immediately associated with the superiority of the 'race', and thus one reads in many books that 'the Asian' was not fully developed, 'the Oriental' had inner limits, and only 'the Greek' was a fully developed human being. Even the Greek gods were more intelligent:

> *'But the Greek gods are also wiser than the barbarian ones, just as the Greek is brighter than the barbarian, indeed they seem wiser to the barbarians themselves than their own gods.'*

Xenophanes, the vagabonding philosopher who roamed the marketplaces with his lyre, became the 'Petrel of the Enlightenment', Pythagoras, with his phobia of big beans, had gathered 'men and women of Greek blood' into his sect and soon brought half of Italy under his control, while Heraclitus, who was up to his neck in shit, invented the 'logos' and the 'supra-personal world principle' before he was mauled by the dogs.

All this can be read in a standard work on the Pre-Socratics by Wilhelm Capelle from 1935, which is still in use today. Thus it says on the first pages:

> '*On the west coast of Asia Minor there is a strip of land which is of greater significance for the intellectual history of the Occident than entire country complexes of the Old and New Worlds put together: ancient Ionia, the home of that branch of the Greek nation over which the good genius of our race had poured out his gifts in truly lavish abundance*'.

It didn't matter what foolish fantasies were concocted, as long as the stories were beautiful. Misters Winckelmann and Hegel cheerfully beckon to us from their graves, while their fantasies just gallop away across the open field. Founding myths combined with the Sea Peoples, the 'noble simplicity and quiet grandeur' and the racist beliefs of the late nineteenth century. So far, perhaps only a utopian fantasy, but it is beginning to smell ugly.

When Eliza Butler, a professor at Cambridge University, published a book in 1935 entitled 'The Tyranny of Greece over Germany', it was immediately banned, this time by the Nazis. She criticised above all the utopian 'Schwärmerei' of German scholars and aristocrats, few of whom had ever visited Greece in the eighteenth and nineteenth centuries.

The Germans' obsessive preoccupation with Greek antiquity had led to a 'tyranny of an ideal' based on 'absolute beauty' rather than truth, and in which logical contradictions were completely ignored. '*In what other country would the discovery of clarity, simplicity and nobility in art have led to such dire results?*' she asked, anticipating what was to come. But such views were not in demand at the time.

Stay tuned, it won't be long now to see what happens when you get a story 'wrong'. We already have the ingredients, we just need to mix them. The dessert is now served with the beautiful phrase that is still served in many books on the history of philosophy:

'From Myth To Logos'.

This saying comes from a book published in 1940 by Wilhelm Nestle, who was later awarded the Cross of Merit of the Federal Republic of Germany. This idea of a development from a purely 'mythical thinking' in the time before 'the Greeks' to a scientifically based 'rational thinking' since 'the Greeks' is itself nothing but a myth that had slowly and continuously been drilled itself into the brains of German philosophers.

From Winckelmann via Göttingen, from the Humboldts to Hegel, a good story never dies out and continues to exist until these days. But it is worth taking a closer look at Mr Nestle's work, for there we read the following:

> *'To walk this path from myth to logos, to grow up from immaturity to maturity of spirit, seems to have been reserved for the Aryan peoples as those of the most highly gifted race, and among them, again, this development can be traced in none as clearly as in the Greeks'.*

Delicious, isn't it? Of course, the Germans were all Aryans - except the Jews, of course, at least according to the Nazis, who were just in power that time. And one has to assume, that they were not the only ones thinking like that.

Enjoy it, because here the completely exaggerated philosophical fantasies about 'the Greeks' are being mixed with the delusions of a completely misunderstood theory of evolution as presented by Wallace and Darwin. This not a new phenomenon, as new findings are frequently adjusted to one's world view; just remember what happened to Newton and his theory of gravitation.

Anyone who carelessly uses this expression with 'myth' and 'logos' should be very aware of the story as a whole. Nestle received his Cross of Merit in 1953, many years after the end of a Nazi dictatorship that had got completely out of hand. But the old stories are very difficult to get rid of. Still today, when Germans hear 'Greek philosophy', they yell 'Here!' and start with rational science. It's something like a Pavlovian reflex that persists to this day. To this day, universities continue to teach the image of 'rational science' that began in Miletus, although they prefer to leave out the ideas of a superior 'race'.

To be honest, the farting philosophers at a symposium with sex, drugs, and a rocking lyre are much more likeable. '*Gut winds need to flow freely*', Krates agreed, the philosopher from the next table.

It should have become clear what can happen when stories are misunderstood. However, it is time for us to leave Berlin and get our minds back on other things. So let's go back in time again and head to a place where a completely different kind of music is playing. Let's go to England, or rather to the British Empire, because that's what it had become in the meantime.

While the French had been occupied with their revolution, and the Germans with their Greeks, England concentrated on the economy and had just changed in the fast lane. The cranky gentleman we are about to meet in London has a completely different view of the world. And to be quite honest, I'm more than happy that now comes a completely different story. So, all on board, next stop is London...

Stories from Islands

Present - Not Voting

At almost every university, faculty meetings are in general pretty boring, and everyone tries to avoid these bureaucratic nightmares somehow. However, there are also some rare exceptions. At the University College of London, for example, a respectable figure has regularly attended these events for over one hundred and fifty years, and is usually recorded as 'present - not voting' at the votes, which is in itself a considerable improvement to some of his colleagues who tend to be noted for 'voting - not present'.

The name of this remarkable colleague is Jeremy Bentham, the godfather of this university, one might say. He dedicated his body to science after his death, but on the condition that it would be preserved and displayed in a cabinet at the university.

Since then, his head was used more than once for the morbid amusement of younger students and had to be replaces in the meantime. Nevertheless, he still sits enthroned in one of the university's cupboards. Even though this quirky Englishman is only known to a few people, his ideas and writings had a decisive influence on the thinking and acting of modern society.

Bentham was born in 1748, at about the time Rousseau started his erotic affair with his 'maman'. He was one of those wunderkinds you would do well to avoid. In an age at which normal mortal children begin to learn to no longer pee in their pants, little Jeremy already spoke Latin. With twelve he started his law studies, completed his bachelor's degree with fifteen and his master's degree with eighteen. However, as he grew up in a rather wealthy family and law did not suit him at all, he decided not to work at all, and instead took up the latest sciences of his time and began to write.

According to many of his contemporaries, he was an absolute weirdo, and even Goethe called him a 'most radical fool'. Bentham, in fact, advocated among other things the freedom of speech, the ending of slavery and the abolition of the death penalty. That alone was not all that unusual. But beyond that, he also demanded the separation of church and state, equal rights for women, and campaigned against the criminalisation of homosexuals. He was therefore really quite a strange contemporary.

But the reason for his timeless fame is another story altogether. Bentham published his 'Introduction to the Principles of Morals and Legislation' in 1780 and opposed all the writings of the Enlightenment known up to that time. Instead of talking about reason and mind, as was common at the time, Bentham stood before his audience and claimed that people seek pleasure and avoid pain. If you really want to understand people and their actions, then everything could be subordinated to this statement. Full stop. That's all you need. No statements about morality, freedom, religion, nation, nothing like that. That was pretty damn radical.

Later, he called this principle of the greatest happiness 'utilitarianism', and provides a definition right in the first lines of his book, probably to make the reader happy.

> *'Nature has placed mankind under the governance of two sovereign masters, pain and pleasure. It is for them alone to point out what we ought to do, as well as to determine what we shall do. On the one hand the standard of right and wrong, on the other the chain of causes and effects, are fastened to their throne. They govern us in all we do, in all we say, in all we think...'*

Pleassure and pain, right and wrong, cause and effect. He was a quite radical enlightener. If all people seek pleasure and avoid pain, then of course a government has a special role to play, namely to ensure the maximum happiness for its citizens. There is a very simple formula for this: '*The greatest happiness for the greatest number of people*'. And what is the best way to measure happiness? Money, of course. And here lies the radical explosive power of the whole idea, perhaps in a completely unexpected way.

If one were to take away a pound sterling from a rich person, it would make that person just a little bit unhappier. And if one were to give this pound sterling to a poor person, it would make him much more happy. Both together are in sum a lot happier, so on balance there is more happiness than before. If you take this game further, you quickly realise that you are in the middle of the ever-present debate about fair tax rates and distributive justice.

Of course, this idea of 'utility' has been taken even further by many of his colleagues, so what now follows is a very brief summary of a basic economics course, part one, Fundamentals. Don't worry, it's quite simple:

Imagine you are all alone in the world with only two products, bread and wine. Since it is all about happiness, you can imagine that you are just as happy with ten bottles of wine and one loaf of bread as with three loaves of bread and three bottles of wine or ten loaves of bread and only one bottle of wine. At times you may have more of one thing, but less of the other. But whatever the combination is, you are always equally happy. To become really happier, you would need to have more bread and more wine at the same time. But that is not possible as you are alone in the world.

However, fortunately one day you meet someone who is also only having bread and wine. You now start to trade with this person. You might have ten bottles of wine and one loaf of bread, but your new fellow villager has ten loaves of bread and only one bottle of wine. You start trading bread for wine, wine for bread, back and forth, and behold, and at one point you might have five loaves of bread and six bottles of wine, and your new friend has six loaves of bread and five bottles of wine.

Five loaves and six bottles of wine are definitely much more than three loaves and three bottles of wine. So you are happier than before, your new friend is happier than before, and now you are having a huge party because you have just passed the basic economics course, part one. This is how markets work, at least according to the theory, and how it is still taught in any university today. You may now introduce some nice words like 'Pareto optimum' and the 'law of diminishing marginal utility' to make it sound a bit smarter, but it won't change much about the basics.

Bentham, just laid out the foundations of our current economic system even before the French Revolution. The guy really had a quirk, as Goethe and many other of his contemporaries put it. However, he did not yet have a clue about marketing, advertising and social networks. Today, the advertising industry knows very well what people want and what makes them happy. Sometimes even much better than the people themselves know. And the algorithms of certain companies can even work out quite precisely what will make people happy next week. You usually don't even know what you want tomorrow, but some algorithm has already ordered today what you want next week. What this has to do with free will, the question whether 'pleasure and pain' alone are the sovereigns of your decisions, and how all this fits together with Bentham's ideas, is something you must find out for yourself.

Immanuel Kant, Bentham's counterpart from Königsberg, already saw that free will is not so far off. Although he also had no idea about advertising and algorithms, he knew the married couples from his neighbourhood and saw what happened to the free will in a marriage. '*O wonderful such harmony, that what he wants, that wants she...*'. He probably had a good point there.

Kant saw a fundamental problem with 'utilitarianism'. If Bentham says that everything is subject to utility, then it doesn't matter how you reach your goal. Consequently, the purpose justifies the means. 'It is for them (pleasure and pain) alone to point out what we ought to do, as well as to determine what we shall do', writes Bentham. According to him, happiness and unhappiness also determine how one should act.

Kant saw a major problems in the argument in which apparently something was morally 'right' merely because several people, or even the majority, wanted it. He was concerned with the moral justification of one's own actions, and according to him, this does not depend on maximising happiness or minimising harm alone. Not only is the majority always right in its decisions, but the ideas of happiness and unhappiness themselves may change over time.

Kant therefore sought for universal moral principles, for respect for the human being 'as an end in itself', which should apply as a maxim for action.

> *'Act only according to that maxim whereby you can at the same time will that it should become a universal law.'*

Kant formulated his 'categorical imperative', an almost devastating critique of utilitarianism, set out in the 'Groundwork of the Metaphysics of Morals', published in 1785, five years after Bentham's book. Reading Kant is a real challenge in itself, not only because of his style of writing. However, his influence remains undisputed to this day, especially when it comes to universal principles such as 'human dignity' and 'human rights'.

To illustrate the problem we do another little thought experiment. Only this time it's not about bread and wine, but about a driverless railway carriage that is hurtling towards five track workers. The track workers can't hear or see you, and you have no way of warning them. Unless a miracle happens now, the five track workers will die. So far, so good.

Fortunately, you are standing at a switch that can divert the train to another track. All you have to do is press a button and you can spare the lives of the five workers. Unfortunately, there is also a worker on the other track bed, whom you cannot warn either. If the purpose justifies the means, you divert the wagon, save the five track workers and sacrifice the sixth. Five is more than one, 'The greatest happiness for the greatest number'. Many will likely vote that way.

Now imagine a hospital where five track workers are desperately waiting for a vital organ transplant to survive after a terrible accident with a driverless railway carriage. Two need a kidney, one a liver, one a heart, and the fifth a lung.

And now, purely by chance, a young, perfectly healthy athlete arrives at the hospital, having just twisted his foot during training. All his organs are in perfect condition and he fits perfectly for the transplantation. Five is still more than one, but does 'the greatest happiness for the greatest number' apply here too?

Is it really justifiable to sacrifice one person to save others? And what happens, if this sportsman is your husband, your friend, your son, a loving father of five beautiful children?

This whole debate is basically about moral dilemmas and justice. These are still highly topical issues, even more than two hundred years after Bentham and Kant. Regardless of which area of society is at stake, these two different perspectives are the lynchpin of the disputes. So let's leave the two disputants to their own devices, because it's about time we changed the venue.

Time is a good topic anyway, because it was still assumed that creation began on a Sunday, you remember? This deepest conviction has not changed yet. So finally, let's deal with the problem of 'time' and go to Edinburgh in Scotland. All aboard, we're in a bit of a hurry. We have to get there before ten o'clock, otherwise it will be dangerous on the roads. You remember, because of the sudden showers....

Enlightenment in a kilt

Welcome to Edinburgh. First let's sit down in a pub, order a good old Scotch whiskey and see who's hanging around here, while the barman is pouring a dark, syrupy liquid called ale into a large mug, which doesn't even attempt to develop a frothy crown.

England only had three universities at that time, Cambridge, Oxford, and in the third one Jeremy Bentham loitered in the cabinet. By contrast, tiny Scotland, with its five universities, had become one of the intellectual centres of Europe in the middle of the eighteenth century, and with David Hume, Adam Smith, and James Watt, there were just three figures sitting at the next table who were causing an uproar throughout Europe. James Hutton, the fourth of the group, was still missing. He was probably staring at his stones again and had forgotten the time.

David Hume was arguably the foremost sceptic of his time, and as with many others, he was concerned with the certainty of knowledge. While Descartes had demanded to use one's mind, Hume even doubted the mind. He was quite down-to-earth, already reasonably corpulent and actually managed, as one of the few people, to create a healthy economic basis for himself through his writings.

Hume was interested in how the human mind works at all, and was probably one of the first scientific psychologists in world history. He expressed doubts that one can really rely on one's senses, since knowledge is only based on experience. We see, for example, how the sun rises in the morning and sets in the evening. We also know that it will rise again tomorrow. But we can't really prove scientifically that it does so tomorrow again?

Whoever was thinking this way and questioning everything was by nature messing with the Catholic Church who is based on 'faith', and of course Hume was a true atheist. For him, all the religious ideas about a God, the creation of the world, the stories of the Deluge, were pure speculation and had nothing to do with secure knowledge. Above all he was taking issues with his colleagues, who were more speculative about the knowledge than taking human beings as they actually are, he argued.

> *'If we take in our hand any volume; of divinity or school metaphysics, for instance; let us ask, Does it contain any abstract reasoning concerning quantity or number? No. Does it contain any experimental reasoning concerning matter of fact and existence? No. Commit*

> *it then to the flames: for it can contain nothing but sophistry and illusion.'*

In any case, the idea that one must be very careful with the certainty of knowledge was not entirely absurd. Until Albert Einstein, people were convinced that time and space were unchangeable; since then, we have known about black holes, curved spaces and relative time. And some people still believe that all knowledge began with the Greeks, or that the world began at eight o'clock on a Sunday morning. Thus, one cannot be certain even of secure knowledge.

Concerning Adam Smith, he had just invented the new national economy with his book 'Wealth of Nations'. It was not the ownership of land that was accountable for the wealth and prosperity, he argued contrasting the prevailing view, but it was the workers in the new factories who contributed to the general wealth of a nation.

Smith thus not only describes the transformation from an agrarian to an industrial society, but is still considered one of the founders of classical national economics, in which every citizen of a country contributes to the national income and thus to the national prosperity through his or her economic actions. This happens completely independently of whether it is intended by the citizen or completely unintended - as if done by an 'invisible hand'. This is the only time and in the only context - in book four, chapter two, in the middle of paragraph nine - that the concept of an 'invisible hand' is mentioned in this book.

Strangely enough and in particular these days, many liberal economists hold Adam Smith's book and his concept of an 'invisible hand' as the bible of capitalism. They derive a whole dogma from it, demanding the withdrawal of the government from the economy, its full deregulation and the unhindered free play of market forces. However, they neglect the fact that almost all market regulations in almost all sectors of the economy originate from initiatives of the industry concerned.

Furthermore, Adam Smith had never called for the economy to be left to itself or to be deregulated. On the contrary, he argued that a true 'free market' only works if all market participants have full access to information and all obey the same rules. You will have to find out for yourself how this can be reconciled with reality. But that's the way it is with Bibles, most of the time they are not read, but they are believed.

The third member of the group, James Watt, was already quite drunk and unresponsive. His head laid motionless on the table, making soft hissing noises. James was dreaming of huge steam engines. He had finally received his patent, and today was a day to celebrate. Watt had been commissioned some time ago to repair a steam engine made by Thomas Newcomen. He improved it immediately and received his patent No. 913. From then on, Watt's new steam engine was to drive the industrial revolution, and it did so very diligently.

The same year that James Watt received his patent, his colleague Nicolas-Joseph Cugnot, who was about the same age, presented the world's first automobile in Paris. The seven-metre-long wooden tricycle with a huge water tank in front of the handlebars could the hardly be steered, however, so that after twelve minutes the first car accident in world history occurred when the vehicle 'crashed' into a wall at walking speed. They had simply forgotten to apply the brakes.

Anyway, let's leave this illustrious group, which will surely have a hard day tomorrow. You still have the image of Mr Ussher in your mind, I hope, and now let's start slowly to undermine that image of an earth created some six thousand years ago. That's why we've come here to Edinburgh in the far north.

Looking into the abyss of time

Let us move on to number four of the truly great Scottish enlighteners. This man had been staring at the stones on his sheep farm for nearly fourteen years. After years of observation, it finally must have dawned on him that stones just don't want to grow. And with this quite simple insight, he all of a sudden shook up the biblical view of history.

James Hutton was supposed to become a lawyer, but during his university studies at the age of seventeen he was rather absent-minded and much more interested in chemistry. Therefore, a short time later, he started studying medicine, as this subject had the closest links to chemistry. Law, theology and medicine were still the standard courses of academic education in Scotland. However, he probably never worked as a doctor later on, but instead he and his old friend from school invented a technique to produce ammonium chloride artificially. This venture earned him enough money to retire to the country and to start working with his stones.

In the meantime, people knew from mining, among other things, what the world looked like below the surface, and that there were always very specific layers of rock, mineral deposits and coal seams. All over Europe there were heated arguments about how these stratifications came about and by what they were caused. Hutton theorised that rocks were formed in the earth's core, piled up, folded and eroded away. Whatever was eroded was carried by rivers to the sea, where it was deposited again. There, the material was finally caked together again into new sedimentary layers by the pressure of more and more deposits above them.

His opinion was in stark contrast to the common doctrine taught by Abraham Gottlob Werner in Freiberg, among others. According to this theory, all minerals were dissolved in the oceans after the Deluge and now, as they were gradually deposited, formed the individual layers of the earth. It was a theory that was in full harmony with the Bible. Young Alexander von Humboldt had also been a student of Werner in Freiberg at the time. On his subsequent trip to the Americas, he searched the Andes, looking among other things for these clues that could confirm Werner's strata theory. A futile endeavour, as we know today.

In summer 1788, James Hutton and two fellow scientists were sailing along the east coast of Scotland in a small boat and soon reached a spot called Siccar Point. Hutton could not believe his eyes when he spotted the rock formation. It was exactly what he had been looking for the last few years, the proof of his theory, for which he had been ridiculed and berated from all sides.

He had already seen many rocks and sedimentary layers, not only on his farm, but all over Scotland. People said he preferred to read from rocks rather than books. At Siccar Point, however, 'the mind seemed to grow giddy by looking so far into the abyss of time', said one of his friends who accompanied him.

What Hutton saw at Siccar Point in June 1788 were horizontal and vertical layers of earth that gave him a glimpse into the past. First, horizontal sediments formed in the sea. They became folded and then eroded after the land had risen above sea level, until only the vertical layers remained standing. Again the land was flooded, new deposits formed horizontally above them, and again the land mass had risen above the sea and was exposed to erosion. A continuous, constantly ongoing process that required one thing above all: time, and a hell of a lot of it.

'The result, therefore, of our present enquiry is, that we find no vestige of a beginning, no prospect of an end'

he noted in his book 'The theory of the earth', which also made him one of the founders of modern geology. Completely unintentionally, Hutton, who was actually a religious man, had messed with the church, and criticism and reproaches hailed from all sides. For the following years he was busy proving and defending his theory in detail.

James Hutton had discovered the time. An infinite amount of time, in fact. Certainly, even he did not realise that it would eventually be about four and a half billion years of Earth's history. But he knew and showed that the barely 5800 years of an Archbishop Ussher would be far from sufficient to allow sedimentary formations to grow in this way.

There was no end to this geological development, no completion of an age to be expected, and in his era this ultimately meant that there was no God.

Today we know that the upper sandstone layer at Siccar Point is about three hundred and forty-five million years old, whereas the lower vertical layer is four hundred and twenty-five million. It is truly an impressive glimpse into the past, no doubt about it.

And those who needed all this time to explain their theory, many years after Hutton, were Alfred Russel Wallace and Charles Darwin. But we are not there yet.

First, let's look at how much belief in the Bible and in the story of the Deluge was still deeply rooted in people's minds.

Homo diluvii testis

Despite the Enlightenment, the Bible, the story of creation and the Deluge remained the core of thinking at that time. The majority of the population was firmly convinced of the stories in the Bible, and there was no question about it. Everything was good, everything was beautiful, and perhaps the creation would soon be fulfilled. And if not, then they had just made a little mistake with this 'a thousand years are one day'. So what, man is fallible. But the numerous fossil findings were the scientific proof of the Deluge, people were convinced, even if there were some sticking points that didn't really fit into the picture at all. So let's take a brief look at some of these strange-looking stories.

The Dutch humanist Johannes Goropius Becanus, for example, as well as the French scholar Bernard Palissy, were subject to public ridicule in the sixteenth century when they both claimed that extinct animal species were behind the fossil finds. But it was as clear as day, and everyone knew, that it had to be the giants that were already mentioned in the Bible.

'*There were giants in the earth in those days; and also after that, when the sons of God came in unto the daughters of men, and they bare children to them, the same became mighty men which were of old, men of renown*' (Genesis 6.4).

Moreover, the African church father Augustine had already confirmed this when a fossil tooth was brought to him over a thousand years ago. And if the church father Augustine said so, then that was true.

The two discoverers also had a somewhat peculiar reputation. For while Goropius suspected the biblical paradise to be near his home in Belgium, Palissy spent sixteen years unsuccessfully imitating Chinese porcelain, burning everything he could get his hands on, including the sofa and the wooden floor of his house. Instead of the finest Chinese porcelain, he produced rather crudely rustic-looking pottery that still bears his name today.

A few years later, around 1613, a fossil skeleton measuring eight and a half metres was unearthed in the Dauphiné region of France. It was initially assumed to be that of Teutobochus, the giant king of the Kimbers and Teutons, who were so devastatingly defeated by the Romans in the Provence in 102 BC.

The remains were taken to Paris in a triumphal procession, where the surgeon Habicot and the anatomist Riolan later got into a heated dispute about whether the remains were a biblical giant or the fossilised remains of an elephant from Hannibal's campaign. In a never-ending controversy, some one hundred years later, the Benedictine Augustin Calmet was called in as an arbitrator, an excellent expert not only on current questions about angels, demons and ghostly apparitions, but also on witchcraft, vampirism and the resurrection of the dead.

Calmet was able to confirm that, according to the Bible, there had indeed been giants, but that they had all perished in the Flood. That seemed to end the discussion about fossils for the time being. However, it was not until the last century that it was finally confirmed that the fossil was a deinotherium, an elephant-like proboscidean of at least one million years of age. Unfortunately, the fossils found in the Dauphiné at that time are now considered lost.

Among the interpretations of the Deluge story, there were some extremely curious ideas. Thomas Burnet, for example, in his 'Telluris Theoria Sacra', the sacred history of the earth, referred in 1681 to a passage in Genesis: '*In the six hundredth year of Noah's life, in the second month, the seventeenth day of the month, the same day were all the fountains of the great deep broken up, and the windows of heaven were opened*', the Bible reads on the day the rain came (Genesis 7.11).

Burnet interpreted this to mean that the antediluvian paradise was a flat world without seas or mountains. Under the earth, however, there was supposed to have been water-filled caverns. When these caverns collapsed, the water that gushed out was supposed to have triggered the Flood. The idea of underground caverns filled with water quickly became popular and was widely discussed in the learned circles of society.

Only a few years later, in 1696, William Whiston, published his 'New Theory of the Earth'. Like Edmund Halley, who had previously discovered Halley's Comet, Whiston was convinced that the Deluge was caused by a comet five thousand years ago. Halley himself calculated the Deluge to have occurred in 2342 BC on the basis of the comet. Whiston now claimed that the earth had passed through the moist tail of a comet, whereupon the rain exerted strong pressure on the earth's crust, whereupon it finally broke, and whereupon the 'fountains of the great deep' poured over the earth. His work was highly praised even by Isaac Newton.

This theory of water-filled caverns was taken to the extreme by the Swiss Johann Jakob Scheuchzer. He presented a skeleton he had found as that of a man drowned in the Deluge, a 'Homo diluvii testis', and was hailed by experts for his findings.

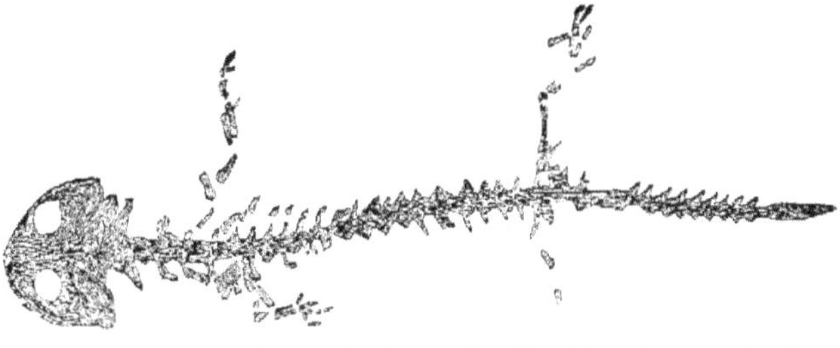

FIG. 42.—Skeleton of a gigantic Salamander (*Cryptobranchus scheuchzeri*) from the Upper Miocene of Oeningen, Baden; one-tenth nat. size. "Homo diluvii testis" of Scheuchzer. (Wall-case 19.)

However, much later it turned out that it was merely an extinct giant salamander. According to Scheuchzer's theory, published in 1726 in the Philosophical Transactions of the Royal Society, the 'fountains of the great deep' broke open by the hand of God. The Lord had laid his hand directly on the Earth's axis, which abruptly stopped the Earth's rotation, causing the water from the 'fountains of the great deep' to spill over the globe, similar to the morning cup of coffee when you accidentally bump into the table while still drowsy.

In the same year, a completely different discovery attracted attention. Johann Beringer, professor of medicine and personal physician to the Prince-Bishop of Würzburg, was a passionate collector of fossils. In his "Würzburger Lithographien" he reported on strange fossil stones that had come into his possession within the last year. On them were images of copulating frogs and wine pigeons, but also Hebrew characters and shooting stars.

Beringer was one of the most renowned scholars of his time. He described the total of two thousand stones as undoubtedly genuine and considered them to be relics of the Deluge. Of course, the hoax was soon exposed, but to this day it is unclear whether the ageing professor himself was not behind the whole story. After all, around three hundred 'Reichstaler' went to the bearers of the stones, about three times Beringer's annual income.

Throughout Europe, however, people stubbornly stuck to the Bible's account, even though geological findings and fossil finds increasingly contradicted it. The earth and its inhabitants were only a few thousand years old, and all fossil finds were the result of the Deluge, so it was written, and so it was supposed to be. The creation story, the Fall of Man and the Deluge were the dogma of that time, which no scientific discovery, no matter how significant, was able to undermine. Instead, there were repeated attempts to reconcile the latest discoveries to this dogma.

About giraffes

By the year 1800, some ten million people were living in the British Isles and the Industrial Revolution was slowly gaining real momentum. When Queen Victoria, the great-great-granddaughter of George II, finally ascended the throne in 1837, an entire age would be named after her by the end of the century. By the end of her reign in 1901, the population of her United Kingdom had grown to almost forty million. Malthus had written his work a hundred years earlier and could only have guessed how enormous the population growth would be.

Meanwhile, more and more mineral resources were needed, geologists became increasingly important, and the more and the deeper the digging, the more frequently fossils were found that always occurred in very specific layers of the earth. By the time James Hutton died in 1797, he had not yet been able to convince the experts of his ideas. Instead, attempts were made to develop ever new theories about the origin of the world that could bring religious ideas and scientific knowledge into line with each other.

Scheuchzer's 'homo diluvii testis' was only debunked as a giant salamander in 1811 by Georges Cuvier. Cuvier was a professor at the College de France and a member of the Göttingen Academy of Sciences. He advocated the widespread thesis that species were unchangeable and that one or more catastrophes occurred in early times that wiped out many living creatures.

At the same time, Jean-Baptiste de Lamarck wrote his 'Philosophie Zoologique' in 1809, the first attempt at a theory of evolution, half a century before the findings of Darwin and Wallace.

According to this theory, certain characteristics should be passed on to the next generation, such as the length of the neck in a giraffe or the hind legs in kangaroos. Lamarck imagined that animals would need to use some organs more, and others less, as a result of changing environmental conditions. In the course of time and through the frequent use of certain organs, such as the frequent stretching of the neck in giraffes, the neck lengthens and this characteristic is passed on to the next generation. According to this theory, all animals were still created by God, but had the capacity to change over time and to develop certain characteristics.

Another characteristic of his theory was that the evolution always proceeded in a specific direction. Thus, his theory not only explained why animals change, but also showed that evolution always takes place from a simpler system towards a more complex one. Evolution therefore had a special meaning and a purpose, thus still representing the old thinking.

It was precisely this idea that later led Robert Chambers to claim that the 'white Caucasian' was superior to all other 'human races', and which later appeared in a similar form in the 'Aryan Herrenrasse' in the National Socialist era. It fitted beautifully into a view of history that was also held in 'Germany'. It was the idea that the original forms of life evolved into ever higher beings. With Chambers, the miracle of divine creation became a religious version of Lamarck. Again, with minor modifications, it was possible to hold on to the biblical world view and the story of the Deluge.

Meanwhile, the scientific findings became increasingly clear. Only now was the field of philosophy really beginning to separate itself from the natural sciences. Up to now, philosophy had been understood to include everything that had to do with human beings in some way, including what is today understood to be the natural sciences, but also history and philosophy. Gradually, the educational reforms of Humboldt, for example, became apparent.

From this point on, scholars increasingly specialised in individual areas of science, concentrating their attention on very specific questions, only to realise that with every answer, new questions arose. This was the moment when 'natural philosophers' became real 'natural scientists'.

After Jean-François Champollion succeeded in deciphering the Egyptian hieroglyphs in 1822, a whole new front opened up against the biblical story of creation. All of a sudden, there were dated documents. Assuming that the dates were correct, things must have happened very quickly in Egypt after the Deluge, and people must have been very, very fertile. The same was true for all the other advanced civilisations in India, China, and Latin America. Something about the biblical chronology just doesn't add up.

For this reason, many people were delighted when the first excavations in Mesopotamia finally brought good news, namely that all the information in the Bible was correct. Or nearly correct, as anyone can make a mistake. However, the Epic of Gilgamesh was still lying in the cellar of the British Museum, waiting to be discovered.

The collecting frenzy of museums was now at its peak. Like Aristotle, museums collected and catalogued everything they could get their hands on. There were not only piles of boxes of material from the excavations, such as those of Emile Botta, Henry Layard and his colleague Hormuzd Rassam from Mesopotamia. Thousands and thousands of preserved animals and plants also accumulated in the cellars and showcases, and were examined and scrutinised by scientists. The demand for ever new specimens was inexhaustibly great.

The Swedish Carl von Linné had already described and classified more than seven thousand plants in the middle of the eighteenth century. The way he went about it is still the standard today. Now more and more new finds were being added from all over the world, and collectors like Russel Wallace, whom we will come to in a moment, were even able to make their living from it. However, the sheer quantity of animal species collected so far, of beetles, butterflies and other insects, of snakes, reptiles and small and large mammals in the museums made it clear that not everything could have fit on Noah's ark, not even a thousand arks would have been sufficient.

Lamarck's ideas were now helpful for the time being, and gave a purely rational explanation entirely in the spirit of the 'Enlightenment'. Everything was created by God in the beginning, and then species could evolve. And if the giraffe only stretches its neck long enough for the uppermost leaves in the tree, then its neck will also grow. Again everything was explainable, again everything fitted into the Bible story. You always find exactly what you are looking for.

And now with Wallace and Darwin there were two explorers who took a look outside the cone of light of the street lamp to find the key. The great diversity of species was to lead them on a whole new trail. However, this story required time, a lot of time, an infinite amount of time. It could no longer be brought in line with the descriptions in the Bible. Only a few thousand years were not enough. Millions of years were needed. We' ll get to the rest of the story now.

So let's go aboard the Beagle and join Darwin as he discovers his theory of evolution on the Galapagos Islands. He did so, didn't he? So here we go, off to port, the ship is already waiting for us...

Sailing the Pacific

Charles Darwin was still a rather inexperienced youngster when, at the age of barely twenty-two, he was offered to join the voyage of the HMS Beagle in August 1831 as a 'scientifically educated companion'. Darwin had studied natural sciences extensively and was familiar with Alexander von Humboldt's travelogues as well as Lamarck's theory on the variability of animal classes. He had taken Hutton's work and other books on geology with him for the voyage, which was estimated to take about four years and was to serve the accurate mapping of certain coastal areas of South America for the British seafaring.

It was certainly not an easy job, as apart from the seasickness, such a long ocean crossing, even if it sounds tremendously exciting, is first and foremost one thing: endlessly boring. The first captain of the Beagle, Pringle Stokes, had committed suicide in Rio out of sheer boredom, so Robert FitzRoy had to take over for him and bring the ship home safely. On his second voyage, FitzRoy now feared a similar fate for himself as the new captain of the Beagle. At least Darwin managed to dissuade the captain from similar suicidal thoughts for the next five years. A few years later, however, the captain committed suicide by cutting his own throat with a razor. But back to Darwin.

When the Beagle left England in December 1831, Darwin had no idea the journey would last almost five years. Wherever possible, he tried to go ashore and make his own explorations. Anyone who had ever been at sea on a small sailing vessel for more than three weeks knows to appreciate extended shore excursions. Life on board is about as pleasant as a permanent stay in a youth hostel. One sleeps in shared rooms without the slightest privacy, while the hostel is moving up and down and people vomit their food more often than expected.

It took almost four years for the Beagle to finally reach the Galapagos Islands and only stayed there for four and a half weeks, until the islands had been sufficiently surveyed. Darwin was twenty-six and after eleven days of crossing from the coast of South America, he was glad to go ashore again. The volcanic islands, however, did not have much to offer at first glance. Each of them was different in some way. Sometimes densely overgrown with jungle, others rather bare without almost all vegetation. However, if there was one thing Darwin certainly didn't do, it was to throw his arms up in the air and shout loudly 'Yay, I've discovered the evolution'. Quite the opposite was the case.

The somewhat clumsy-looking blue-footed boobies and the frigate birds with deep red throat pouches probably caught his eye immediately, as did the many sea seals in the water and on the beach, where iguanas can also be found in the rocky areas. Huge land turtles can be found in the inland, while a colony of small penguins cavorts in the water alongside huge shoals of fish. Penguins at the equator can only be found here, nothing has changed in that respect.

However, there is no such fascination in Darwin's record. After five years, even a paradise can become boring. Nicholas Lawson, the deputy governor of the Galapagos Islands, had to draw Darwin's attention to the different species of turtles. By the shape of their shells, Lawson told him, one could tell exactly which island they came from. At that time, however, Darwin did not attribute any further significance to this fact.

He also had no idea what exactly he was putting into his boxes when he started collecting birds. It was not until he returned to England that an expert, John Gould, pointed out to him that the finches he had caught were so different from each other that they were actually twelve different species.

The most exciting experience for the twenty-year-old in the Galapagos Islands was probably watching two of these giant turtles mating. The sight was a little absurd and he almost felt sorry for the animals. The two turtle shells pushed against each other, making noises like those of a gouty castanet player, and the male rattled like a lung patient on the first ascent of Mont Ventoux.

Darwin was rather clueless during his stay in the Galapagos Islands. He observed iguanas, rode a turtle down the slopes, packed it aboard the Beagle as travel provisions and finally sailed away in the direction of Tahiti. Back in England, he published his travel diaries and was first to become famous for his geological observations, such as the formation of coral reefs.

For the next few years, there was absolutely no idea of a theory of evolution, and Darwin did not comment on it either. Whether he spent the next twenty years preparing the book based on the discoveries of his few weeks on the Galapagos Islands remains one of the unresolved details of the story. In the end, however, it doesn't matter, because his book on the theory of the origin of species was to become one of the most important works of his century.

The story of the flying orang-utan

Despite ever new observations and ever better technical possibilities, the view of the world changed only slowly, if at all. People stuck to what they had learned and tried to fit all new discoveries into the old world view. It was due to this sticking to the old convictions that the visions and explanations became more and more absurd and fanciful. An example of this is the story of an initially small provincial newspaper that would soon go down in history.

On 25 August 1835, the New York Sun reported on the latest astronomical discoveries of John Herschel. At the time, Herschel was in South Africa, where he was making astronomical observations with a huge telescope. His father Wilhelm Herschel, who was actually from Hanover, had discovered the planet Uranus and had been honoured for it by his sovereign George III, the King of England. John was to follow in his father's footsteps, had already discovered the Magellanic Cloud, and had become a renowned astronomer worldwide.

It was also a time when new astronomical discoveries were made on a daily basis, and so the report in the New York Sun surprised no one at first. The article had everything that was expected from a scientific article of that time, including many references to the latest research, to other scientists and much more. Thus, it immediately began to report on the divine creation that can be seen in all the new discoveries.

The article reported on the 'realities of a future state' and the kingdom of God, that could be detected in all the discoveries. People were creationists at that time, at least most of them, even in scientific circles. Ussher was still present, as was Lamarck. There was also a very detailed account of the new telescope, weighing more than seven tons, that John Herschel had just set up in South Africa. An apparatus that could achieve a magnification of six thousand times and observe details which had never been seen before. After finding more and more new stars and nebulae, this telescope was now to be pointed at the moon, the article stated. The name Herschel and new astronomical discoveries guaranteed the full attention of the readers in any case.

The next article, the following day, reported that crystal blue lakes and vermilion mountains had first been discovered on the moon, which could also be precisely located. Trees became visible, and Hershel himself reported of brown quadrupedes and lead-coloured unicorns with goat's beards. Grey pelicans and black and white cranes were also sighted before a wall of clouds moved in front of the telescope's lens, making further observation impossible.

In the meantime, the articles in the New York Sun had come to the attention of others, the first articles appeared in other newspapers in the United States, and the first calls reached the editor of the newspaper.

The third article spoke of the 'philosophical patience' with which one had been waiting for better weather. With the aid of the new hydro-oxygen magnifiers, Doctor Herschel had now discovered plains comparable to those in the US, where far more quadrupedes and unicorns were to be found. In the meantime, Herschel had been able to classify thirty-eight different species of trees, nine species of mammals and five species of marsupials. The most exciting was probably a horned bear carrying its young one in its arms. The news of life on the moon now spread like wildfire. Herschel, of course, had a telescope with a resolution hitherto unavailable to any other scientist. The descriptions and precise details of the lunar surface and its craters, the accurate survey with all the distance information were just so convincing that it all had to be true. Newspapers all over the country were now reporting Herschel's discoveries on the moon.

The Friday edition reported new discoveries again, of giraffe-like creatures, white as ivory and a head with two curved horns that resembled a sheep. And finally, Doctor Herschel announced that he had discovered human-like beings, with copper-coloured hair, just over a metre tall, with yellowish faces, some of them with wings like those of bats. This was undoubtedly the work of the Creator, Herschel argued, this was proof of the existence of God.

The circulation of the small paper skyrocketed, the telephones no longer stood still, and even the first scientists now asked whether they could not gain an insight into the records of the reports. In addition to precise geographical information, the newspaper also brought drawings of the creatures. The story now spread across the Atlantic to Europe.

The Saturday edition then also reported on oceans that had been discovered on the moon. Using Gx-lenses, one could see all the crystalline beauty of God's creation, even discovering a small Garden of Eden on the lunar surface.

The following Monday, finally, the paper reported the first temples sighted and happy, very human-like creatures eating orange-like fruit and grinning contentedly as they participated in worship services in groups. Unfortunately, the report from South Africa broke off on the same day. The night before, Dutch farmers and 'domesticated Hottentots' had woken up the doctor and reported that the 'Big House' was on fire, where the technical equipment was installed. The telescope was also affected, and further observation of the moon and its inhabitants was no longer possible for the time being, the newspaper reported.

What was supposed to be a hoax now made waves in America and Europe. Many readers foolishly believed the stories about flying orangutans, goat-headed unicorns, sheep-headed giraffes and happy praying creatures who peeled their oranges themselves. Not just John Herschel's name, but also the unconditional belief in the Bible were widespread, and the ideas of a Bishop Ussher were considered law.

It took a long time for the newspaper to finally expose the hoax and admit that it was nothing but a fake story. Herschel himself was quite amused by the whole affair when he returned from South Africa. He had really been there, which was probably the only thing that was true about the whole story.

The subject of the farce was actually a Mr Thomas Dick, and an attentive reader would have noticed this immediately. That Thomas Dick was a best-selling author from England who sold all the latest discoveries in astronomy, Greek philosophy, biology and geology in his books as God's grandiose creation.

Authors like Thomas Dick, and Robert Chambers a few years later, had no problem at all with incorporating the latest scientific discoveries into their theory of creation. It was a time when the gullibility of many people seemed to have no limits, a time when an Edgar Allan Poe wrote his 'Incomparable Adventure of a Certain Hans Pfaall', who flew to the moon in a tethered balloon, and a time when Washington Irving wrote his 'History of the Life and Voyages of Christopher Columbus', which is why many still believe today that Columbus had to convince the members of the Spanish Inquisition not to fall off the disc at the end of the world. Wonderful, completely absurd stories that some still believe today.

The new version of the creation story had probably begun quite unselfconsciously with Carl von Linné, who catalogued his seven thousand plants in the mid-eighteenth century. The conviction that all the animal and plant species living on the planet could be so wonderfully classified, as Carl von Linné had introduced, led many people to believe that everything had a wonderful order. And if everything was in such wonderful order, then it could only have come from the Creator. So the wonderful idea of 'creationism' was born, in which so many people even today believe with all their fervour.

A few years after the New York newspaper hoax, Robert Chambers wrote his book on the 'Traces of the Natural History of Creation', in which he described the 'Caucasian' as the highest type of human being, and all other 'races' as inferior. Chambers was a creationist to the core. Such uniformity in structure was only possible if there was a Creator behind it, he thought, and so did the many other creationists who abounded at the time.

'*The whole plan is as symmetrical as the blueprint of a house or the design of a man-made garden*', and this blueprint originated from God. Somehow, people could not get this idea of creation out of their heads, which had been burned so deeply into their brains for centuries.

To this day, many people still believe in 'intelligent design', the modern form of creationism. Nowadays, however, people prefer to leave out the reference to the Bible so that the nonsense sounds more scientific. Nevertheless, many research projects are still based on ideas of beauty and symmetry, which the researchers themselves know. They care little. And David Hume sends his regards.

Welcome to the Bermuda triangle

Let us rather return to our history and let the next few years pass us by calmly. It is a turbulent time, with Karl Marx and Friedrich Engels complaining about the exploitation of workers in their Communist Manifesto, and revolutions taking place across Europe in 1848.

Layard is just arriving in London, in his luggage tons of clay tablets, statues, and other relics from Mesopotamia, where they had found Nineveh, as they mistakenly believe. Later, he is on his way to his new employer, the British Museum, and may also have met the now very famous Charles Darwin there, who spent the last few years honing his scientific career, which was progressing very well even without the theory of evolution.

Meanwhile, Charles Dickens published his latest book 'David Copperfield', in which little David is sent by his cruel stepfather to a factory in London at the age of nine to finally earn money. Another young boy, George Smith, on the other hand, was already fourteen when he was taken out of school and starts an apprenticeship in the printing shop very close to the British Museum that printed Charles Dickens' books. From now on, he will spend every lunch break admiring Layard's finds from Mesopotamia.

So let's leave this seething London and head west to the Bermuda Triangle. Not that things are necessarily calmer here, because another ship has just sunk. However, it wasn't one of those mysterious incidents you always hear about. This time the ship was simply torched because the captain was stupid enough to load a cargo of highly flammable oil right next to the galley where open fires were being handled.

When the fire spread on board, there was just enough time to escape to the lifeboats. In one of these boats there was a rather desperate young man who was constantly trying to get the water out of the leaking boat with a coffee mug.

The young man's name was Alfred Russel Walace. He had just lost all his belongings, including his diaries and all the records of his journey through the

Amazon. All his work of the last four years, the entire, completely catalogued collection of beetles, frogs and all the other creepy-crawlies he had been supposed to procure for the museum, was burning right before his eyes. In a cloud of black smoke, some charred remains of his butterfly collection rose to the sky one last time, just before the ramshackle wooden barge reared up once more and sank before his eyes with a loud hiss and bubbling.

Museums were now paying handsomely for new exhibits, for brightly coloured butterflies, whimsical beetles, exotic birds, for animals large and small. Wallace had fulfilled his dream. He had always had to earn his own living, working as a surveyor, builder, watchmaker, teacher and whatever else. But as soon as he had the first hundred pounds, he set off for South America with his friend Henry Bates to collect new animal species for a museum. Now in his thirties, he paddled in a rowing boat towards his total financial ruin. Never again in his life, he vowed, would he set foot on a ship if he survived this. He should.

Back in England, Wallace had taken lodgings with his sister Fanny; he himself was a bit of a slob at the moment, one might say. Some parts of his collection had fortunately been sent to England before him on another ship, and the revenues at least covered the expenses of his journey. His agent in London, who sold his collections on to the museums, was actually quite pleased with his work. Fortunately, this agent had even insured the cargo of the ship from which Wallace had just managed to escape in the Bermuda Triangle.

When Wallace received the two hundred pounds of the insurance money at his sister's house, he was already making new plans. There were now hundreds of collectors in South America, hunting for ever new species and subspecies of beetles and butterflies.

To make really good money, Wallace had to go to a part of the world that was still little explored, and yet promised rich pickings. The tropical island chain between Singapore on the mainland in Southeast Asia and Australia, the Malay Archipelago as it was then called, seemed just right to Wallace for his venture. It was literally at the other end of the world, and it was unlikely that he would meet other collectors there. So let us join him in this faraway paradise, for what he found there was tremendous.

The Malay Archipelago

Wallace was to spend eight years in the archipelago between 1854 and 1862, criss-crossing the islands and regularly sending new collections of beetles, butterflies and other species to his agent in London, which brought him a tolerable income. He later noted three hundred and ten mammals, one hundred reptiles, eight thousand and fifty birds, seven thousand and five hundred shellfish and one hundred and ten thousand and four hundred insects in his travelogue 'The Malay Archipelago', which he published after his return. But what he actually discovered was much more formidable.

By the time we come across Wallace in Borneo, he has collected thousands of insects. He noticed that the beetles, butterflies and whatever else he had collected always differed just a little bit from each other. Also, they all lived together in a relatively small space. From this quite simple observation he formulated his first law:

> *'Every species has come into existence coincident both in space and time with a pre-existing closely allied species'.*

All this was still perfectly consistent with the views of Lamarck. Wallace, however, had also noticed some other things. On Borneo he had seen the first orangutans and described them quite lovingly in his book before he skinned them and sent the carcass to London. Apart from these forest people, for that is what orangutan means in Malay, he also got to see his first orang belanda, the 'Holland man', a nose ape jokingly named by the locals after the first European 'longnoses' they got to see.

On the islands further to the east, kangaroos inhabited the trees, but no monkeys. He found the same with other animal species. In the east animals were found that originally came from Australia, in the west those that originated in Asia.

Such a distribution only made sense, however, if at some time the islands in the west had been connected with Asia, and those in the east with Australia. Monkeys would have arrived from Asia, kangaroos from

Australia, and there was no connection of land in between. In fact, this biological dividing line between Australia and Asia still exists today and bears his name: the 'Wallace Line'.

The raising and lowering of the sea level corresponded exactly to the observations Hutten had made at Siccar Point after years of watching the stones growing. Again, Wallace's first law, that new species evolve from closely related species, was confirmed.

Thus Holland Man evolved from apes in the West, the tree kangaroo from kangaroos in the East. Thus, geology and time must have played a huge role in the origin of species. Although it was now clear that species evolved, Wallace could not explain why they did so.

He also noticed that the individual species produced many more offspring than were necessary for their survival. If all the offspring would survive, the world would be completely overcrowded within a short time. So, he sat down, started to calculate, and came to the following result:

> '*A simple calculation will show that in fifteen years each pair of birds would have increased to nearly ten million! whereas we have no reason to believe that the number of the birds of any country increases at all in fifteen or in one hundred and fifty years. With such powers of increase the population must have reached its limits, and have become stationary, in a very few years after the origin of each species. It is evident, therefore, that each year an immense number of birds must perish—as many in fact as are born.*'

The observation was similar to the one Adam Smith had already made when he observed the pretty children near the barracks, most of whom did not live past the age of fifteen. Nevertheless, Wallace did not want to come up with a striking idea. He couldn't think of anything else but butterflies and bugs.

Usually, you need a 'time-out' to get your mind off things. In Wallace's case, it was a mosquito that bit his buttocks, infected him with malaria and sent him to bed with violent attacks of fever. His brain shut down for the time being. It's like rebooting the hard drive when the programme hangs. Although Wallace had not yet known a computer, the effect was the same.

During the fever attacks, he remembered what Malthus had said on the subject of overpopulation and the 'struggle for existence' for food. He had warned at the time that people were multiplying more than they could keep up with food production. With this idea, Wallace's observations began to make sense. Parents produce vast numbers of offspring. The siblings differed a tiny bit from each other. The environment remained the same, the food supply remained the same, and eventually only the offspring that were best adapted to their environment survived. All others were severely decimated or perhaps died out completely.

But this evolutionary pressure was not only evident within a species itself, but also between them. As soon as one species was better adapted to its habitat than another, it pushed the latter back and perhaps even completely overtook its place. Species thus come into being and species pass away in a completely natural way and without the intervention of a creator.

The immense explosive power of these findings was obvious, because ultimately this concept could be used to calculate back to the origin of life. It was a constant, continuous development that eventually reached back to the beginning of time. The few thousand years of a Mr. Ussher, however, would by no means be sufficient for this process.

Moreover, it was a continuous development that was still ongoing, and would continue to do so in the future. The idea that man was the crowning glory of creation, that something at all would be fulfilled at some point and come to some completion, was thus also passé. Everything developed from something that pre-existed, there was always something that existed before, and there will always be something that will follow. In his feverish delirium, Wallace had discovered the two main pillars of the origin of species: variation and natural selection.

Thus, Larmarck's thesis was wrong in some fundamental points. According to him, the 'original giraffe' had always existed, or better, a creator had made it. For him, and many of the creationists who followed, creation developed in a very specific direction, it was directed towards a goal, a specific 'purpose' and resulted in a higher 'meaning'. We have already seen where this view can lead if you get the stories wrong with Robert Chambers' 'white Caucasians' and Nestle's phrase 'from myth to logos'. So you don't even have to be a creationist to hold some of these absurd views. Old beliefs last a long time and keep adapting without really disappearing. But back to the story at hand.

In any case, Wallace dispelled this idea over a hundred and fifty years ago. According to his theory, successive generations always varied a little from their parents. These variations were completely random, in no way directed towards any goal, they did not even have to make sense, and they did not serve any higher purpose. Rather, the environment, and only the environment, determined which offspring should survive with which variation.

A hedgehog can have developed such beautiful spines against its predators over thousands of generations, but if the environment changes and a lorry drives over it, all that remains are ugly spots on the road. Its spiked coat is of no use at all. Which variations a descendant gets is determined by coincidence, and which variation survives is determined by the environment, which can also change. It is a system that does not allow any predictions. There is no goal, there is no purpose, there is only 'cause and effect'.

With Wallace, Darwin and the theory of evolution, we are thus back in the midst of the old argument between 'meaning and purpose' and 'cause and effect'. Ultimately, Wallace's reasoning followed exactly the same thinking that began with Descartes. Switching on one's brain and using this massive organ under the fontanel can lead to some really interesting insights. You really don't need to be a professor to do this, a butterfly collector on Borneo was quite enough.

After Wallace finally recovered from his malaria attack and feverish delirium, he wrote his short, world-famous essay entitled 'On the Tendency of Varieties to depart indefinitely from the Original Type' and sent it to Charles Darwin with the request that he forward the paper to Charles Lyall. Lyall was the most respected geologist in England at the time, he too was a creationist and believed in Lamarck's thesis, but slowly began to doubt it after this letter.

Darwin must have been shocked when he read Wallace's letter. In the end, it was an abridged version of his ideas on just a few pages, and he probably couldn't have written it better himself, he later said. However, he now saw before him another scientist with almost identical results. Lyall and Darwin decided to present both papers, one by Wallace and one by Darwin, in parallel to the Linné Society in London on 1 July 1858. Finally, the following year, with Wallace still travelling in Asia, Charles Darwin published his world-famous work 'On the Origin of Species'.

It was obvious that the principle of 'variation and natural selection' contradicted many previous beliefs. But the argumentation of Wallace and Darwin was clear and unambiguous. Thousands of generations were needed for a new species to emerge from the smallest variations, and millions of years were needed for a human being to emerge from the first primordial cell, according to this new theory of evolution. Millions of years were also needed to build up the individual geological layers of the earth that Hutton had studied and in which the fossilised remains of this development lay buried.

It was quite understandable that many people went to the barricades, and the criticism was harsh, not only from religious circles. Bishop Wilberforce of Oxford accused Darwin of blasphemy. The principle of natural selection was absolutely incompatible with the Word of God, he wrote, and contradicted the clear relationship of creation to its Creator. The bishop was right, indeed, but in a different way than he actually intended.

Darwin and Wallace had a lot to listen to, and for a long time to come people would not believe them. When Darwin died in 1882, he was buried alongside

Isaac Newton in Westminster Abbey. The significance of his writings was no less influential than Newton's. Similarly to the discoverer of gravitation, it was to take decades before the views of Wallace and Darwin finally became accepted. Shortly afterwards, Wallace's book 'Darwinism' was published, which ultimately coined the future name of this new theory.

> '*Darwin wrote for a generation which had not accepted evolution, and which poured contempt on those who upheld the derivation of species from species by any natural law of descent*', Wallace noted in the preface of his book.

However, the theory of evolution suddenly found support from a completely different region. There, a discovery was made that would provide evidence for the origin of species. All you had to do was to read the newspaper. Reading sometimes helps, even if this small local newspaper was certainly not known to everyone. But the place really has it all. Come with me, I'll invite you for an early morning beer. Just what you need right now. Let's go to Barmen...

Of beans and flatheads

It's hard to believe that the Galapagos Islands in the South Pacific, long-nosed monkeys on Borneo, and the small town of Barmen on the Wupper in Germany could have anything in common. Nevertheless, let's go to the little kiosk on the market square and order a beer early in the morning, as is so common here sometimes. Until recently, Barmen was actually quite a peaceful place, but now the chimneys of the new factories were steaming and sooting up the airways. But we don't need the beer for that alone. A good drink is also necessary when we take a look at the back pages of the small local newspaper. It is the issue of 9 September 1856, and there we find the following article:

> *'In the neighbouring Neanderthal, the so-called Gesteins, a surprising discovery has been made in recent days. Through the breaking away of the limestone rocks, which admittedly cannot be regretted enough from a picturesque point of view, one reached a cave which had been filled by clay mud in the course of the centuries. When this clay was cleared away, a human skeleton was found, which would undoubtedly have been disregarded and lost had it not fortunately been saved and examined by Dr. Fuhlrott of Elberfeld.*
>
> *According to the examination of this skeleton, especially of the skull, the human being belonged to the family of the flatheads, who still today inhabit the American West and of whom several skulls have been found in re-*

cent years on the upper Danube near Sigmaringen. Perhaps this find will contribute to the discussion of the question: whether these skeletons belonged to a Central European primitive people or merely to a horde that was roaming (with Attila?)'.

It is always amazing what finds can be made in the remoteness of the provinces. However, the article and the corresponding find it describes would probably have remained completely unnoticed had it not been consulted by a scientist from Bonn who had been working on human history for some time. Only two years ago, Hermann Schaaffhausen, so the scientist's name, had himself written a short paper 'On the permanence and transformation of species'. It was not only in the distant Malay archipelago that Darwin was being closely pursued. Schaaffhausen no longer believed in Bishop Ussher's story of almost six thousand years of human history either. Mankind must have needed at least a hundred thousand years, he thought.

In any case, Schaaffhausen identified the remains as those of a prehistoric man. He had thus finally proved a daring hypothesis that he had already voiced earlier. On 4 February 1857, about one and a half years before the writings of Wallace and Darwin were presented to the Linné Society in London, the scientist announced before the 'Niederrheinische Gesellschaft für Naturheilkunde' in Bonn that these bones were the primeval remains of a human being who had long since died out today. It was the proof of a theory that Darwin was to publish years later in his Descent of Man.

The avalanche he set off with this assertion was understandable. Schaaffhausen, however, stuck to his assertion and defended himself with a hymn to science, *'with which it has thrown down error and prejudice, it moves conqueringly over foreign territories, and if one represents its path, it can invoke its ancient right, for all the science of the ancient world has emerged from it'*.

There it is again, the science of antiquity. Hermann Schaaffhausen had grown up in 'Germany'. He no longer believed in the calculations of Bishop Ussher, but the ancient Greeks were burned deep into his brain stem. He was quite sure that everything had started with them.

After Wallace and Darwin had already published their work, Charles Lyell came to Bonn to examine the findings. He confirmed Schaaffhausen's results and William King finally gave the remains his scientific name 'homo neanderthalensis' in 1864. It was thus undisputed and officially confirmed that the Neanderthal man was an early form of the human being. Evolution did not only exist in the animal kingdom, but also in humans. Shortly afterwards, Darwin published his book on the descent of man.

In 'Germany' however, people fought tooth and nail against this view. The most famous German pathologist of his time, Rudolf Virchow, had looked closely at the fossils in 1871 and insisted that it must have been a person suffering from rickets, but that it was certainly not an early human being. It simply cannot be what is not allowed to be. An opinion that was held until Virchow's death in 1902, the year in which the young Professor Delitzsch gave his lecture on the Deluge story in Berlin. Old convictions are difficult to discard, and sometimes it even takes centuries for some findings to get around.

Ten years after the discovery of the Neanderthal, Gregor Mendel suffered a similar fate as Georg Grotefend with his cuneiform writing in Göttingen. Darwin and Wallace were able to explain the origin of species with their theories, but they had no concrete answer to how this mechanism worked. They had no clue about genetics or chromosomes as carriers of genetic information.

Mendel did nothing but do a little statistics. He took a lot of time, carried out various experiments and began to calculate. In 1862, he began with some crossing experiments on peas, which he documented very precisely. Four years later, he published his 'Mendel's Rules', which showed how certain traits can be passed on through generations. He thus became the father of modern genetics, but no one was interested in his results, because until then no one had imagined that Mendel's vegetables could have anything to do with human beings apart from severe flatulence. Except perhaps Pythagoras, who seems to have had a bad premonition even then.

It was not until more than thirty years later that his experiments and rules were to be recognised as the fundamental findings of modern genetics. After all, genetics was also used to prove the theory of evolution. So if you go back in history long enough, today you can even prove the relationship between them and the cherry tree in your garden. The fact that Mendel was ironically a Catholic priest and abbot of St. Thomas near Brno is another one of those staircase jokes of history. But like Georg Grotefend, Gregor Mendel was the right man, in the right place, only the time was not yet ripe for him.

It's time we slowly came to the end. The last journey will take us to the past and to a city where an unfinished and still ongoing story took place.... so to say...

He who saw the abyss

Of false rabbits and mouse-dogs
Ark of a Dream

He who saw the abyss

We have almost reached the end of the story. In the meantime, we have travelled halfway around the world and been on the road for many thousands of years. I had invited you on a colourful journey to the origin of the stories that are still being told, and many things should have become a bid more clear, one would hope.

Some ancient stories have been preserved until today. With the Christian faith and the Catholic Church, they were introduced to Western Europe and determined the life and thinking of the population for many generations. Other stories originate more from the imagination of some scholars a few hundred years ago, but these have also survived and still shape our ideas of the past and our identity.

It is fair to say that the Enlightenment demystified a world view that existed for centuries. This development began with people like René Descartes, who called for people to believe less and instead use their minds properly. Isaac Newton brought the heavens down to earth, thus destroying rather casually the conviction of a God-given order of above and below, with far-reaching consequences on the structure of society as a whole. People were supposed to free themselves from their self-inflicted immaturity by using their own minds 'without the guidance of someone else', as propagated by Immanuel Kant.

The medieval concept of 'meaning and purpose' was slowly replaced by the search for 'cause and effect'. The advances in medicine, technology, economics and all other fields were tremendous. When Wallace and Darwin came up with their theory of the evolution of life, when the mysteries of the Bible were revealed, the world seemed largely enlightened.

It would have been so nice, one would think, because at last all the enlightenment would have made sense and served a certain purpose. But that is not how the world is working, as we have seen on our journey. There is only 'cause and effect' to explain the world the way it is. 'Sense and purpose' only exist in the imagination of men, and of that they have a whole lot.

The Age of Enlightenment was at the same time responsible for the creation of numerous new myths that are still believed in today. History was invented, connections were constructed and many scientific or allegedly scientific findings were misused for a new world view. The story of the Sea Peoples was fabricated, as was the fantastic idea that all thinking began with the Greeks. False myths were told and national identities were made up that never existed in this way. One believed in the superiority of the own 'race', in the higher destiny of a 'nation', in divine providence and a hidden world plan.

In this boiling pot of ignorance and false conviction, people were racing full steam ahead into the delusions of the modern age. Everything had to have a higher sense, everything had to have a greater purpose. That's how it had been learned, that's how it should be. The battles of times long past continued to be fought, the newly created nations were invoked and oversized monuments erected.

Two world wars and decades of ideological warfare with millions of victims later, in the second half of the twentieth century, it seemed as if the goal had finally been reached. The world had changed enormously. One flew to the moon, explored the planets of the solar system, could cure or at least alleviate most diseases, and had deciphered the genetic code of life.

At the beginning of the 21st century, the world was seen with completely different eyes. They had learned from the past and finally considered themselves in an enlightened world. One should have thought so. They were so very wrong, as you may see from the last story.

Of false rabbits and mouse-dogs

Whoever has a brain should use this gift, and not just carry it as an extended spinal cord between the shoulders
(Albert Einstein)

This story takes place at a time when many people began to believe in an imminent doom again. After all, one was living in a very special time, felt accordingly special, and of course something very special had to happen. The past is filled with such beliefs, and we have already encountered some of them on our journey. This story begins on 30 December 2019 with a young ophthalmologist called Li Wengliang in a hospital in Wuhan, a Chinese 'small city' of about eight million people. He managed to identify a new 'disease' with the naked eye. He was certainly far ahead of his time and a very exceptional representative of his guild. However, that is how the story goes.

Over the following weeks, the experts announced that all of this was nothing new and no cause for alarm. Anyone who claimed otherwise was a right-wing conspiracy theorist and had no idea about science. A few weeks later, the very same experts tied cloth rags around their heads and proclaimed the end of the world. Anyone who claimed otherwise was a right-wing conspiracy theorist and had no idea about science.

While some people still rubbed their eyes in disbelief, the public was bombarded with more and more bad news and the dawn of a new age was proclaimed. The old was sold as completely new, autonomous thinking was condemned as sacrilege, scientific evidence was regarded as treason, and scepticism as a lack of faith.

In no time, a new religion had arisen whose disciples wrapped cloth rags around their heads and believed in the end of the world. People followed their false gurus and prophets who preached eternal damnation and a sudden death while selling their letters of indulgence. Salvation, they preached, was only by injection.

Actually, however, it was less about an ominous disease than about an 'organisation' that had almost infinite funds at its disposal, or rather kept the key to the treasure. One just had to do it the right way to get hold of them. As is well known, immeasurable wealth creates covetousness, which is why soon some 'sponsers' came forward who were only too happy to help and whose help was gladly accepted. The invitation to the buffet was delivered and the guests poured in hungrily. All they had to do was to help themselves.

After the young ophthalmologist from China had done the groundwork, a Mr Ferguson from Imperial College in London stepped up to the scene. He was known worldwide for his colossally wrong predictions beyond all reality, which is why he had also become one of the most important advisors to the 'organisation'. So it came as no surprise to anyone that his predictions once again unerringly landed in a parallel universe. The 'sponsors' were happy, the organisation announced the end of the world, and so the 'battle of the buffet' began.

The whole story reminds of a mixture of 'Till Eulenspiegel' and the 'citizens of Schilda'. When Hermann Bote wrote his work 'Till Eulenspiegel' half a millennium ago, he probably had no idea that one of his stories would have such a topical reference.

In his 53rd history, Bote reports 'How Eulenspiegel sewed a living cat into a rabbit skin for the furriers in Leipzig and sold it in a sack as a living rabbit'. The deceived furrier, who had bought the proverbial pig in a poke, firmly believed that he had '*bought the most beautiful living rabbit he had seen in years*'. He and his colleagues only realise the fraud when they let the false rabbit be hunted by their dogs and it escapes up a tree and starts meowing. But by then Till Eulenspiegel was already long gone. '*I thought there was no fool in the world but me*', Hermann Bote had his Till Eulenspiegel exclaim 500 years ago. '*But now I see that the whole town is full of fools'.*

Not much seems to have changed. Even today, the experts believe in rabbits that climb trees and meow. Well, even the dragon slayers of the Middle Ages believed in the existence of dragons.

As entire economies were ruined and existences destroyed, this farce was increasingly reminding of the fall of the city of Schilda, also a story from the 16th century and astonishingly up to date. The wise men from the town of Schilda were the most demanded advisors at the courts of the time. They were in such demand that they had already stopped returning to their homes, which forced their wives to give them an ultimatum.

After a specially convened council, the burghers, in their almost immeasurable wisdom, agreed to become stupid as hell for that they could stay at home with their wives and children. '*Whatever foolish thing comes into the mind of anyone, that he should do*', they decided unanimously. And they were damn good at being abysmally foolish.

After folly had taken hold everywhere, the chronicle of the town reports of its own demise, mice roamed the streets of Schilda, as there were no cats, and no one knew how to control the plague. One day a tramp came into town with a cat under his arm. When asked what he was carrying, he told the inhabitants that it was a mouse-dog and sold it to the citizens for a lot of money. Soon the inhabitants feared that this mouse-dog would also eat cattle and people, so they set fire to every house in which they suspected the mouse-dog to be, and thus burnt down their own town. Anyone who suspects an analogy to the present day is quite right.

After all, the burghers left their burnt city, '*settled in many places and planted their breeding far and wide*', the story of Schilda ends some five hundred years ago. And their descendants still tie cloth rags around their heads today, one might add today.

Over three hundred years of enlightenment were gone. Darwin and Wallace did somersaults in their graves, the pale shadow of Immanuel Kant walked though Königsberg pulling his hair out, and searching for his mind, Descartes and Rousseau plunged together into the floods of the Mediterranean, and the Newtonian universe collapsed under its own gravity into a black hole. Only David Hume kept smiling, for he had been proved right again. It was so easy to be immature. People believed again in flying orangutans and meowing rabbits climbing trees.

You will find out for yourself how the story will end. Our journey through the stories of time ends here, and I hope you enjoyed the trip though some five thousand years of hi-stories. Maybe there was the one or the other souvenir for you.

It is always worth asking since when people started telling each other what kind of stories. When you know where they come from, the answer sometimes surprises you all the more. You can believe them or not, it is entirely up to you. But I will say goodbye to you now - although I do have one more, as a kind of dessert, to take your mind off things.

Ark of a Dream

The story of the Ark is not over yet. In 1985, a gentleman named Douglas Simmonds entered the British Museum. He had a clay tablet with him, which he presented to Irvin Finkel. Although a fairly young Assyriologist at the time, Finkel immediately recognised the value of the tablet, for in the very first lines of the tablet he read the following: '*Athrahasis, listen to my advice, that you may live forever. Destroy your house, build a boat, leave all your possessions behind, and save lives*'.

Finkel, however, could not persuade Simmonds to give him the rare find straight away, and so another thirty years passed before this clay tablet fell into his hands again. It turned out to be a rather old version of the Epic of Gilgamesh and the story of the Deluge.

In the meantime, however, Finkel had become a professor and a lot more mature when the tablet came back to him again. With his long, snow-white beard and grandfatherly looking eyes, which he hid behind round glasses, he increasingly resembled a modern, very sympathetic version of the biblical Noah.

The information he unearthed while translating the text contained detailed instructions for the construction of the ark. The author of the tablet not only specified the shape, but also the size and quantity of materials to be used. The frames of the ark were thus made of wood, wrapped with rope and sealed with bitumen. The dimensions were gigantic. Not only would several forests have had to be cut down to build it, but a rope of five hundred and twenty-seven kilometres in length would have been needed to wrap around the frames.

Of course, the professor, with his pride as an Assyriologist, could not resist making a replica of the ark, even if only to scale. To the professor's surprise, the Ark was not, as it is still assumed today, a ship with a bow and stern, possibly even equipped with a rudder and sails. The depiction of a ship with a house on top was terribly wrong. Rather, the ark was circular, as the only thing it had to do was floating. And so, today, we have a fairly clear idea of what an Utu-napishtim or a Noah on his ark might have looked like to those around him.

Selected literature

Adams, Douglas
The Hitchhickers Guide to the Galaxy, 1979
Aristophanes
Die Wolken, 423 v.Chr.
Bentham, Jeremy
An Introduction to the Principles of Morals and Legislation, 1780
Boccaccio, Giovanni
Il Decamerone, ca 1350
Bottéro, Jean
Everyday Life in Ancient Mesopotamia, 2001
Bougainville, Louis-Antoine
Vayage autour du monde, 1772
Burkert, Walter
Die Griechen und der Orient, 2003
Capelle, Wilhelm
Die Vorsokratiker, 1935
Chardin, Jean
Voyages en Perse et aux Indes orientales, 1686
Dalley, Stephanie
Myths from Mesopotamia, 1991
Darwin, Charles
Voyage of the Beagle, 1839
Darwin, Charles
On the origin of species, 1859
Defoe, Daniel
A Journal of the Plague Year, 1722
della Valle, Pietro
Reiß-Beschreibung in unterschiedliche Theile der Welt, 1674
Descartes, Rene
Discours de la Methode, 1637
Diogenes Laertios
Leben und Lehre der Philosophen, ca. 3.Jh
Finckelstein, I./ Silbermann, N.A.
Keine Posaunen vor Jericho, 2015
Finkel, Irvin
The Ark before Noah, 2015

Geary, Patrick J.
The Myth of Nations, 2002
Hamel, Debra
Der Fall Neira, 2004
Hayes, Christine
Introduction to the Bible, 2012
Herodot
Historien, ca. 430 v.Chr.
Hobbes, Thomas
Leviathan, 1651
Homer
Odyssee, 8. Jh. v.Chr
Homer,
Ilias, 8. Jh. v.Chr.
Hume, David
An Enquiry Concerning Human Understanding, 1748
Hutton, James
Theory of the Earth, 1785
Kant, Immanuel
Grundlegung zur Metaphysik der Sitten, 1785
Kant, Immanuel
Was ist Aufklärung, 1784
Layard, Austen Henry
Niniveh and its remains, 1849
Lindner, Joachim
Mordfall W, 1978
Malthus Thomas
Essay on the Principle of Population, 1798
Mac Sweeney, Naoise
Foundation Myths and Politics in Ancient Ionia, 2013
Michaelis Johann David
Fragen an eine Gesellschaft Gelehrter Männer, 1762
Niebuhr, Carsten
Beschreibung von Arabien, 1772
Niebuhr, Carsten
Reisebeschreibungen nach Arabien und andern umliegenden Ländern, 1774
Platon
Der Staat, ca. 380 v.Chr

Platon
Timaios, ca. 360 v.Chr.
Platon
Phaidon, ca. 380 v.Chr
Rauwolf, Leonhart
Aigentliche Beschreibung der Raiß, 1582
Raspe, Rudolf
Baron Munchausen's Narrative of his Marvellous Travels and Campaigns in Russia, 1785
Roth, Martha T.
Law Collections from Mesopotamia and Asia Minor, 1995
Rousseau, Jean-Jaques
Du contrat social ou Principes du droit politique, 1762
Sandel, Michael,
Justice – What's the right thing to do?, 2009
Schrott, Raul
Gilgamesch, 2014
Schrott, Raul
Ilias, 2013
Shapiro, Ian
The moral foundations of politics, 2003
Smith, Adam
Wealth of Nations, 1776
Wallace, Alfred Russel
The Malay Archipelago, 1869
Wallace, Alfred Russel
Darwinism, 1889
Waters, Matt
Ancient Persia, 2014
Wilkinson, Toby
Aufstieg und Fall des Alten Ägypten, 2015
Winckelmann, J. J.
Gedanken über die Nachahmung der Griechischen Werke, 1755
Xenophon
Anabasis, ca. 370 v. Chr.

www.ingramcontent.com/pod-product-compliance
Ingram Content Group UK Ltd.
Pitfield, Milton Keynes, MK11 3LW, UK
UKHW050738150325
5004UKWH00078B/522

9 783754 344859